Praise for _10 Bit_

A bit is defined as a small part of something. _10 Bits of Wisdom_ is anything but small in the wisdom department. John Early shares big chunks of wisdom about life, business, leadership, family, and God. However, he takes these truths out of the classroom and shares them from his life experience in the boardroom, the family room, and the hospital waiting room. John shares his story in such a humble and transparent way that you can't help but relate to it.

John also shares how his life and his understanding of what matters most in life were radically transformed by putting his faith in Jesus Christ.

I highly recommend you read this book!

Alex Rahill, Lead Pastor, LifeChurch, Canton, MI

There is great wisdom in story, and you will not be disappointed with this storyteller! Here is a life that has learned the essence of what is important. He has discovered the key lighthouses to guide us on our journey and has generously made them accessible.

This book is a _tour de force_ of some of the best thinking from the past 15 years, from business whizzes to masters of the spiritual life. John has combined and simmered all of this wisdom, then integrated it into his story that has found not only over-the-top business and financial success, but, more importantly, has discovered the secrets to real and lasting success as a man grounded and centered in God and his relationships with family. This is a wonderful book!

Dr. Tim Hogan, PsyD, LP, CIRT
Director of the Grace Counseling Center, Detroit, MI.
and co-author of _How to Find the Help You Need._

10 Bits of Wisdom from the Shoe Shine Guy

A Transformed Life

John Early

Published by Waldorf Publishing

2140 Hall Johnson Road
#102-345
Grapevine, Texas 76051
www.WaldorfPublishing.com

10 Bits of Wisdom from the Shoe Shine Guy:
A Transformed Life

ISBN: 9781943092376
Library of Congress Control Number: 2015936737
Copyright © 2015

Printed in the United States of America

Dedication

My life has been filled with countless blessings from the Lord, and this book is dedicated to five of the most precious: Janet, John Shay, Jennifer, Mike, and Lucian. I love you all more than words could ever say.

Table of Contents

Preface - A New Beginning

"Do not conform any more to the pattern of this world,
but be transformed by the renewing of your mind."
Romans 12:2

When I first started thinking about writing this book, *10 Bits of Wisdom from the Shoe Shine Guy*, I was thinking about the ten bits from the standpoint of a businessman, someone who had spent 30-plus years in the business world and who could convey some of the attributes that were beneficial to him in his career. That all changed when I actually sat down and began to convey my thoughts onto paper. The ten bits of wisdom: Know Your Purpose, Character, Attitude, Goals, Teamwork & Trust, Respect, Courage, Regrets, Reconciliation, and Grace, all took on a whole new meaning for me. So much so that I had to change the title of the book and add *A Transformed Life*.

How do I begin to explain a transformation? How on earth do I try to explain a *radical* transformation? I can't. There is no way to convey the actual thoughts, emotions, feelings, and nuances that make up the changes that took place in my heart, my soul, and my mind after accepting Jesus Christ into my life. My hope is that by writing all of this down on paper I will be able to give you a little bit of insight into what did occur in my life and that it is absolutely possible in yours.

God's timing is inscrutable to all of us. Why He waited 49 years to bring me to my knees will always be a mystery to me. The fact that He actually waited that long for me to finally reach out and accept His grace tells me that He loves me beyond reason. He loves all of us more than we could ever begin to fathom. I believe that sometimes the Lord will wait until we are at the end of ourselves to reach out and take hold of us. It reminds me of the story that was told by Watchman Nee (an early-twentieth-century Christian teacher and church leader in China) in his book, *The Normal Christian Life*:

> I was once staying in a place in China with some twenty other brothers. There were inadequate provisions for bathing in the home where we stayed, so we went for a daily plunge in the river. On one occasion, a brother got a cramp in his leg, and I suddenly saw he was sinking fast, so I motioned to another brother, who was an expert swimmer, to hasten to his rescue. But, to my astonishment, he made no move. Growing desperate I cried out, 'Don't you see the man is drowning?' and the other brothers, about as agitated as I was, shouted vigorously, too. But, our good swimmer still did not move. Calm and collected, he remained just where he was, apparently postponing the unwelcome task. Meanwhile, the voice of the poor drowning brother grew fainter and his efforts feebler. In my heart I said, *I hate the man! Think of his letting a brother*

drown before his very eyes and not going to the
rescue!

However, when the man was actually sinking, with
a few swift strokes, the swimmer was at his side,
and both were soon safely ashore. Nevertheless,
when I got an opportunity, I aired my views. 'I have
never seen any Christian who loves his life quite as
much as you do,' I said. 'Think of the distress you
would have saved that brother if you had considered
yourself a little less and him a little more.' But the
swimmer, I soon discovered, knew his business
better than I did. 'Had I gone earlier,' he said, 'he
would have clutched me so fast that both of us
would have gone under. A drowning man cannot be
saved until he is utterly exhausted and ceases to
make the slightest effort to save himself.'

Do you see the point? When we give up the case,
then God will take it up. He is waiting until we are
at the end of our resources and can do nothing more
for ourselves.

I tried for so long to have the perfect life without God.
It was like running on a treadmill and someone kept
sneaking up behind me and turning up the speed. I kept

going faster and faster, accumulating more and more stuff, but I still ended up getting nowhere of any real significance. The problem with running on a treadmill for most of your life is that you expect the people around you to keep up, but they not only can't always keep up, most of the time they're not even on the treadmill with you. I thank God for pulling the plug on my treadmill. It was only a matter of time before that belt finally broke and I would have lost the race.

My challenge to all of you is to take a hard look at the treadmill—or the road—that you are currently running on. Is it moving too fast? Is it moving too slowly? Is it even headed in the right direction? I thought for the better part of my life that I knew exactly where my road was headed and precisely how I was going to get there. It took a radical transformation from God to show me where I was in my life, and to allow me to begin dealing with all of the yuck that was inside of me. I have learned that if we don't deal with the yuck that is in our lives, it will deal with not only us, but with all those who come into contact with us as well.

Don't wait 49 years or another minute to start thinking about your life, your family, or your loved ones. Life is not like a Jim Croce song and we can't save time in a bottle.

Time is a precious thing and the older I get, the more I come to fully understand this gift of time. When we take a moment to really stop and think about it, I think we all realize that our days are numbered; we all only have a limited amount of time here on this planet.

My son lost a friend a while ago to cancer. He was 29 years old, married, with two young children. My sister lost her husband and the father of her two children at the age of 39—over twenty years ago. My mom passed away at 63 and my father at 85. Who knows the time that we are allotted here on earth? I certainly don't. I don't think that anybody does. Every day, every hour, every minute, and every moment is a gift—a gift that we all too often take for granted.

Our time is referenced several times in the Bible. In Psalm 39:5, David writes, "You have made my days a mere handbreadth; the span of my years is as nothing before you. Each man's life is but a breath."

And in James 4:14, he says, "Why, You do not even know what will happen tomorrow. What is your life? You are a mist that appears for a little while and then vanishes."

We are a mist. Here for a brief moment and then gone. In the grand scheme of things, we are just a speck. So what does this mean? Why even think about it? It would probably make life much easier not to think about it. But I do. I think about it often. It helps me to focus in on what is truly important. I know that someday my number will be up. I will be called from this place. I will no longer be here on this earth. And that is my conundrum. As much as I am looking forward to spending eternity with Him, I can't put aside the thoughts of wanting to always be with my wife, my children, and my grandchildren. I have to keep telling myself that, as great as it is to be alive and with the people that I love, it will be that much greater with them in eternity. So I refocus and get my eyes back on my audience of One.

I thank Him every day that I wake up. I thank Him for all of the moments that He has given me and for transforming my life when He did. I ask Him to please show me what it is that He needs me to be doing with the time that I do have left.

In Chris Tiegreen's book, *The One Year Walk with God*, he says, "In the grand, eternal scheme of things, we are a small point on the timeline. By the time we learn what we need to know and are equipped to serve, we have but a moment left. But God has given us an awesome privilege. We can accomplish in that moment works of such significance that they will last forever."

Take the time to think about your moments, about the gifts that you have to offer, about your time here on earth. In the movie, *Gladiator*, General Maximus, played by Russell Crowe, speaks to his fellow soldiers before a big battle. He says, "What we do in life echoes in eternity." Think about what it is that you are doing in life. I had to stop and think and reflect deeply on the life that I had before my transformation through the Holy Spirit, and then what it was that God was asking of me after the transformation.

I ran into an old high school buddy of mine about two years ago. We happened to re-connect on LinkedIn and I have been shining his shoes ever since. He started reading my blog on a regular basis and one day mentioned to me that after reading a particular blog on what time we have left here on earth, he kept asking himself a very divergent question: "What are you gonna do about it?" His question pertained to the fact that if we only have a limited time here on earth and given that tomorrow is not promised to us, then what are you gonna do about it? It's a great question that we should all be asking ourselves on a daily basis.

If each moment and every day is a gift, and tomorrow is not promised to me, then what do I do today? How do I treat my wife, my children, and my grandson? How about my friends? What about the new customer who walks into our store? Where do I go? Who do I spend time with? What do I do? Life is zipping by at a pretty good clip. I realize that more of my moments are behind me than what is in front of me (especially after seeing my old high school buddy and realizing that 36 years had just gone by).

How do I figure out what my purpose or reason is for being here? How do I make the best of each moment? I try not to overthink this, but ask God regularly to give me direction. I'm pretty sure I wasn't put here to find the cure for cancer or heart disease. Maybe my purpose is to be the best shoe shine guy there is. Maybe He wants me to use the moments I have left to continue working at being a good dad or husband, to make up for the times I wasn't that person. Maybe it's to be a good grandfather to Lucian—to finally learn how to change a diaper.

All I know is that there is a reason for everything and for every one of us. We all have a purpose and we all have some moments left to make a difference. In one of the most recent *Superman* movies, there is a scene where Superman's father, played by Kevin Costner, has a talk with his adopted son, who is struggling with his identity and purpose for being on earth. He says to him, "Somewhere out there you have another father and he sent you here for a reason. And even if it takes the rest of your life, you owe it to yourself to find out what that reason is." There is still time for all of us to find our reason, if we haven't already, and to make the most of each moment that we have left.

My life was drastically transformed back on January 12, 2008. There was never any doubt about that. I knew that God had gotten a hold of my heart and that my life moving forward would never be the same. What I didn't know, until someone approached me about writing this book, was that God may have big plans for me moving forward, but what He first wanted was for me to take a hard look back and reflect on my past. This was a very cathartic experience for me. I hadn't realized (although my wife, my children, and most anyone else who knew me very well probably had a pretty good idea), that I was bottling up so much inside of me.

He had to reveal the yuck that was inside of me, the stuff I had bottled up over the years. I had put up all of those walls—walls that were supposedly there to keep me safe when, in reality, they were only keeping everybody

10

out. I had to re-think the meaning of Knowing Your Purpose, of Character, of Attitude, and all of the other Ten Bits of Wisdom. Every day now, on a moment by moment basis, I give God my pride in exchange for His humility and grace.

I had to have some hard talks about forgiveness and reconciliation. Not the "hey, sorry for leaving the toilet seat up or the cap off of the toothpaste" kind of talks, but the kind where the tears are flowing and I'm asking Janet and the kids for forgiveness for my absence for all of those years, for not being the husband or the father that I should have been, and for making life all about me.

I had to re-think the relationship that I had with both of my parents, pray that my mom did forgive me in her heart for the quick-tempered and selfish boy that I once was, and take ownership of the fact that the relationship, or non-relationship, that I had with my dad was as much a part of my stubbornness as it was his. I drew just as big a line in the sand as he did, and could have stepped across it at any time.

No, this book took a pretty big U-turn right from the beginning, and ended up not being a book about business habits and attributes, but a book about life habits and attributes. A book about God's long arms reaching out and picking up one of His children and carrying him out of the pit of darkness and despair. A pit that for so long I thought was the place to be and where I felt so comfortable parking myself. In Joel 2:25, the Lord says, "I will repay you for the years the locusts have eaten." He is telling us to let go and not to dwell on the stuff of the past, that He will take care of all of that and will replenish our lives. None of the crud from our past is ours to redeem but is for the Lord to take care of. And He has promised us that He will.

We can all be transformed by Jesus Christ. All we have to do is ask and accept Him into our hearts. For the first 13 years or so of our marriage (I will call this phase I), Janet and I did some really stupid things. Both of us were running at full speed, on separate treadmills, and doing whatever we felt like doing, regardless of the consequences. After Janet accepted Christ into her life (phase II), she was definitely transformed, but our life together became harder. Some of the worst times of our marriage happened during that period of time. The fact that I was being a selfish and unaccepting person didn't help at all.

Then January 12, 2008 happened and God changed both of our lives forever, and moved us into phase III. This has been the best eight years of the 33 years we have had together. That doesn't mean that things are perfect and that we have everything all figured out. We don't. Not every bad thing in our life has a big red bow on it. What it does mean is that we are working together to figure stuff out and that we are on the same road (or treadmill), and moving in the same direction and at the same speed. God is restoring both of us and He has provided the kind of relationship and marriage that He had intended for us all along.

I am blessed beyond measure that my wife and kids still do love me, and, next to God, they are the biggest and most important part of my life. They wanted me to convey the same message: We wanted to let you know that we all learned a lot from the writing of this book, and that it has been a time of continued healing, reflection, forgiveness, and reconciliation. I'm so grateful that the Grace of God has touched all of our lives, and my hope and prayer is that it will touch your life as well.

By taking this journey together, we can all come to better understand the truth. We are not in charge, we are not in control of our own destiny, and we are not alone on this journey. Everything that we have, everything that we do, everything that we become, is because of Him. It is only because of His grace, His mercy, and His love for all of us that we are here.

So walk with me, cry with me, and laugh with me, as I share the ten bits of wisdom from the shoe shine guy.

2 Corinthians 5:17 – "Therefore, if anyone is in Christ, he is a new creation; the old has gone, the new has come!"

My Story

"Moreover, I will give you a new heart and put a new spirit within you, and I will remove the heart of stone from your flesh and give you a heart of flesh."

Ezekiel 36:26

It was a cold, crisp, sunny day in January—January 12th, 2008, to be exact. I was driving down the road on one of the main highways that run east and west, a few miles north of Detroit, I-696. I had just finished playing about three hours of handball in Clinton Township with some of my handball buddies. This had been my regular Saturday ritual for years. I would get up on Saturday morning and make the 35-mile-or-so journey out to the club where all the guys met, and we would play for hours.

I loved handball. Not just for the exercise, but for the camaraderie and the competition as well. The games could be grueling and fearsome. There were no easy games where we would just lob the ball back and forth for the fun of it. Every game was a battle to the end. We tried to annihilate our opponent and take no prisoners. It was so much fun!

After playing on that particular Saturday, I was spent. I sat around and talked to the guys for a while, about what I can't remember (usually it was about who had the greatest shots of the day, which were very seldom any of mine), then I showered up, got into my car, and started the drive back home.

Being totally exhausted and relaxed can have a cathartic effect on a person. I was just heading east on this

16

particular highway, I had the cruise-control on, and my thoughts were wandering… How good it felt to be so relaxed after such a hard workout. What a beautiful day it was outside—cold, crisp, a little sunshine. How great it felt to be alive, and then, BAM!!! I started bawling like a little baby. I wasn't sure what was happening at first; all this emotion was welling up inside of me, and I wasn't a real emotional kind of guy. And then I felt it and heard it. I felt God's presence, the Holy Spirit, fill me up, and I heard myself saying out loud, "I am ready Lord, if you will have me."

I felt like Paul on the road to Damascus when he fell to the ground and heard Jesus call out to him! I didn't know what to do or what exactly was going on. My heart was racing (which was a little concerning because I had had two cardio ablations in the previous couple of years) and I had goose bumps all over. I was looking around, trying to make sure that the other drivers couldn't see me, fearing they would wonder why this grown man was driving down the road, weeping uncontrollably. It was quite a rush to say the least.

I was thinking to myself, *what was that all about? What happened? What do I do now and how am I going to explain this to my wife, Janet?* I can't really remember the rest of the drive home or the countless thoughts that were going through my head. I do remember walking into our house and Janet asking me why I had this peculiar smile on my face and what was going on. I didn't know how to tell her what had just happened. I'm a processor by nature and it takes me a while sometimes to sort through things. This was a pretty big thing that needed some sorting out.

I couldn't quit thinking about any of this the rest of the day and remember not getting a lot of sleep that night. Coincidentally (or was this God's timing at work?), the pastor of the church I attended with Janet and the kids had asked me, a few weeks prior, to give a little five-minute talk on the merits of financial planning. This coincided with the sermon he was giving that Sunday. I had told him I would be happy to do it. I had been attending church with Janet and the kids for several years. This was a way for me to spend time with the family. We would go to church and then out to Sunday lunch and maybe a movie. I was usually more excited about the lunch and the movie, but going to church was part of the package.

I had gotten to know quite a few people at the church and always felt comfortable and welcomed. The pastor, Alex Rahill, had invited me to breakfast on several occasions and would always inquire about my faith. Not in an aggressive or pushy kind of way, but casually and sincerely. I would always give him my standard answer of "Things are good where they are and my life is okay where it is at." We would both chuckle a little bit and he would mention that he would still continue to pray for me "where I was at." I always figured that there was no downside to being prayed for. I would thank him and continue on my way.

There were two services on Sunday: a 9:00 a.m. and a 10:45. The format was that I would go up on stage right after the band had played their worship music and Pastor Alex and I would have a short, five-minute question and answer session about finances. I had a hard time concentrating because of my experience from the day before. My whole body was out of whack and my mind was racing. It was like my days of playing football, and my adrenaline was through the roof. I was running to the bathroom every ten minutes or so and was somewhat concerned about what could happen in front of 200 or so people. I managed to get through the 9 o'clock service just fine (no accidents or mishaps of any kind).

The 10:45 service started out the same. The band had finished and Pastor Alex welcomed me up onto the stage. We did our little five-minute session and he started to wrap up by thanking me and inviting me to take a seat in the audience. I was looking out at the people sitting there and saw my wife and two kids. I wasn't moving. My heart was pounding through my chest and I could feel Pastor Alex trying to pry the microphone from my kung-fu grip. This was not normal or cool. They try to run the service on a pretty regimented schedule and to veer off of that gets everything out of sync.

I looked over at Pastor Alex and asked him if I could just have another minute or two. He graciously obliged (again, he realized I had a kung-fu grip on the microphone). I asked Janet to quickly join me on stage and she came up, a little embarrassed because she thought I was going to ask her to share some of the financial decisions that we make in our household. As she was standing next to me, I looked at Pastor Alex and said that I was ready to take that next step that he had always so subtly asked me about. I was ready to commit my life to Christ.

As those words came out of my mouth, two things happened that I can distinctly remember. The congregation erupted in applause and cheers, and my wife fell to the floor. Janet was so overwhelmed with emotion and thankfulness, because, at that moment, all of her years of praying for me had been answered.

Oh, and there is one other thing that I do remember from that very moment of accepting Christ as my Lord and Savior: my life has never been the same.

***

I attribute my being saved not to a great game of handball (although I do seem to remember that I did play exceptionally well that particular Saturday), but to the presence of others in my life who had a profound effect on me. There was Bob Shirock, the pastor from Oak Pointe Church in Novi where we used to attend church. He was always pressing me about my faith. Not in a fire-and-brimstone kind of way, but in a casual "Hey, John, how's your faith coming along?" kind of way. There is, of course, Pastor Alex from Life Church Canton, where we still attend to this day, who has not only become a good friend but a great mentor for me in my walk and journey in faith. These are men I respect, not only as pastors, but as men of conviction, who stand for something different—something that I was searching for.

The person who has had the biggest effect on me and is the main reason for my searching out Jesus Christ as my Savior is my wife Janet. Not a stronger person of faith do I know. She is a rock, a pillar of strength, and a true disciple

21

for Christ. Janet accepted Christ into her life 12 years before I did. It was not a walk in the park. I did not make her new life easy. If I didn't believe these things, then how could she? I was the Apostle Paul before his conversion, full of ridicule and contempt for something I thought was absurd. The fact that we made it through those years is a testament to my wife's faith and that God does work miracles. Janet did not press me to see things her way. She believed that all things were in God's timing and she was right. God had a different plan for me, and His timing was January 12th, 2008, at around 3:30 in the afternoon.

That is the short version of my coming to the Lord. Let me back up a little bit and fill you in on the early part of my journey through this world and how I ended up on that road on that beautiful winter day.

The Early Years

"We are only here for a little while and
then we are gone."

James 4:14

In the grand scheme of things, we are each but a speck in this giant universe, like a grain of sand on the edge of an ocean that comes and goes, and is directed by the tides. As we go through life, and as we seem to find our place and are beginning to feel comfortable, another tide comes along, moving us in a different direction.

That is not what God has in mind for us—to be moved in one direction or the other by whatever tide happens to come along—but we were not meant to be sedentary either. He wants us to keep moving forward—to keep growing and to keep searching, always with our eyes on Him, looking to Him for direction. We are not to rely on the tides for our direction, but on Him alone.

That is not how it was for the first 49 years of my life. I was being moved by the tides. I was just one grain of sand, lost among all the other grains of sand. I was moving in no purposeful direction. I was just moving.

Life for me began over 55 years ago in Saginaw, Michigan. I was born on March 10, 1959, the fifth of what would end up being nine children (yes, I was stuck right in the middle) to Kathleen (Kay) and William (Bill) Early. My oldest brother was born in 1954 and my youngest sister in 1965. Nine kids in less than 11 years. My mother was also pregnant twice in 1953 and miscarried both times. She delivered a stillborn child in 1966, and miscarried in 1967. She delivered another stillborn child in 1968 and miscarried again in 1969 and 1970. All told, she was pregnant 16 times in 16 years. Her doctor told her that having any more pregnancies could be life-threatening. She finally went and talked to the parish priest. He told her that she had done enough and to get on the pill. That was the beginning of the end of my parents' marriage.

We looked on the outside, to most people, like a nice Catholic family in a nice blue-collar town in the beautiful state of Michigan. I say 'nice' because that is what most people thought about our family. On Sundays we would go to church all dressed up in our finest; nine kids and Mom and Dad taking up the whole pew, everyone behaving very politely, looking straight ahead and paying attention.

I learned from an early age to avoid eye-contact with any of my other siblings during church service. You see, eye-contact could lead to a grin or a giggle, and if that happened, it could set off a giggling chain reaction, which was hilarious at the time, but there would be hell to pay when we got home. That's because Dad was quite strict, and there were a few occasions when the belt would come out. Acting up in church was one of those occasions. Try to imagine all nine of us lined up next to each other and Dad taking the belt to us one at a time. In hindsight, I think being first was the best because you didn't have to listen to the others scream before your turn came up. The anticipation itself could be painful.

Home life was anything but serene. In today's parlance, it would be described as dysfunctional. My father was a hard worker and provided well for the family. My mother was a stay-at-home mom and kept the house in good order. They were both alcoholics. When Dad would start to drink, he would get moody and his temper would start to flare up. Mom would drink to relax and get happy. Not a good combination. My mom was a wonderful cook and would always have a nice meal prepared for dinner. A typical evening in the Early household would be coming home from school, doing any chores that we were assigned, starting in on our homework, and waiting for Dad to come home for dinner. Once Dad got home, we would wait some more. He would typically sit down at the kitchen table and have a beer, then another, and another, and then maybe one more. When he was ready we could eat, but not before. When dinner was over, Dad would start drinking again and continue throughout the evening.

Dinner was eaten in relative silence. We didn't talk about our day. We didn't ask how anybody was doing. We didn't discuss world affairs. We ate in silence, always avoiding eye-contact with Dad. You didn't want to be noticed. You didn't want to give him any reason to lash out at you. He could get physical with you at times, but that was not the worst of it. It was the verbal abuse that hurt the most. His words could cut you to the bone. I learned at an early age to hide or mask my emotions. Emotions were not something to share in our household. They were a sure sign of weakness.

I developed a sense of humor—not to be displayed around my dad, but outside of home, around my friends and schoolmates. I developed a quick wit that could be cutting and, more often than not, hurtful to others. I was not going to let anyone get the best of me when it came to a verbal battle of wits, other than my dad.

My mom was one of the kindest people I have ever known. She never said to me or anyone that I knew a bad word about my dad. If I started to talk bad about him she would shut me down. She held the family together for as long as she could. After our parish priest told her that it was okay to stop having children, the relationship between my parents became even more strained. They finally divorced in 1976, after 23 years of marriage. That was a big life-changing event for me. It was the 1970s and Dad was out of the house. A huge tide had come in and I was going to ride this wave for all that it was worth.

I was a junior in high school at the time of my parents' divorce—seventeen years old and ready to let loose and blow off some steam. I let my hair grow out (almost to my shoulders) and began to drink on a regular basis. This didn't seem unusual to me, because all of the people I hung around with were doing the same thing. What kept me in check at the time was the fact that I had a job—I had worked at one job or another since I was 13—and I played football. I knew that I needed money to do the things that I wanted to do, so I needed to be responsible about work. I also loved being on a team and playing football, so letting myself get out of shape was not an option. Fortunately—or unfortunately, depending on how you looked at it back then—at seventeen, your body can recover pretty quickly. I could work at my job at the school—assisting our school janitor (which is a whole other story that I will touch on later)—and get to the football practices to be ready for the big game on Friday nights. Then I would party all weekend.

There was no more real discipline in our house. Dad was gone and Mom was doing the best she could just to make ends meet. I was the oldest in the house at the time. My four older siblings had moved out, including my sister, who was still a senior in high school.

There are certain periods in your life that you tend to remember more than others, for better or for worse. This was a period in my life that I think of often, and it was not a very pretty picture.

I was angry and hurt. I was embarrassed about the situation that my parents had put me in; none of my other friends had parents who were divorced. All these other families seemed to be like the Cleaver family from "Leave It To Beaver" (which according to Google, was the sitcom that defined the "golly gee" wholesomeness of 1950s and '60s TV), where dad Ward Cleaver always gets home in time for dinner, mom June cleans the house wearing a dress and pearls, and the kids, Wally and the Beav, always learn a lesson by the end of the episode. Looking back, it is easy to understand that what actually goes on behind closed doors is much different than what we see from the outside. I know that nobody has the perfect family. Some of my friends were probably having some of the same issues that we were having behind those closed doors. We put on a great façade for years. People thought that we were a wonderful family—well-behaved children with caring and supportive parents.

When my parents split up, I lashed out in ways that were ugly, selfish, deceitful, and just plain mean, and most of this was geared towards my mother. She got the brunt of what I was feeling. I look back at this time with shame and regret. My mom was one of the kindest, most gentle and unselfish people that I have ever known, and I was making her life miserable, just because I felt bad. She was doing the best that she could just to put food on the table. We went on food stamps and I used to make my younger sister go into the store to buy what was needed because I was too embarrassed.

***

One of the lowest points for me as a person, in regards to how I treated another human being, came around Thanksgiving of my senior year in high school. We were doing a food drive at our school to help out needy families in our community. I grabbed a can of soup or something as I left the house that morning, to take to my homeroom class. The rest of the day at school was uneventful as far as I can remember. When I got home that afternoon, however, the you-know-what hit the fan. I blew a gasket. As I walked in the back door of our home and into the kitchen I saw baskets of food sitting on our table that I realized right away were from the food drive for the needy. I blew up at my mom. How could she embarrass me this way? How could I show my face in school again? What was she thinking?

She was thinking about her children! She was thinking about providing us with a nice meal for Thanksgiving! She was thinking about just getting by! I cringe to this day and get a sick feeling in my stomach when I think about that moment. How could I be so selfish and treat someone so poorly, someone as special as my own mother? Part of the beauty of my mom was that she had the gift of compassion and forgiveness. I'm sure that she was hurting inside, but she was always bigger than that. She had so much love to give, and holding grudges or being angry was not in her.

Someone asked me recently if I ever had the opportunity to ask my mom for forgiveness—forgiveness for not only this one completely selfish incident, but for all of the other times that I most likely came up short as a son. I don't remember ever asking her specifically for forgiveness, but I do remember many times sitting around a table with her and reminiscing about days gone by. She never brought this incident up to me, and looking back on it today, I think that my mom forgave me for this and for all of my shortcomings. That is who she was, and I believe that God put her in my life to show me exactly that, even if it took a full 49 years.

My mom passed away in 1996 at the relatively early age of 63, of brain cancer. From the time of my totally immature and selfish late teen years until her death, when I was 36, we had many great times together. She was happy until the end and brought a smile to everyone's face. She always had kind words to say about anyone and seemed to like everybody.

My wife, Janet, was fortunate enough to be able to be with my mom towards the end as one of her caregivers. She prayed with her regularly and was with her when she gave her life to Christ a short time before she died. I did not understand the importance of that at the time, but now know that my mom has a place in heaven and that we will see each other again. It's funny how sometimes you don't know who your role models are in life, until they are gone. My mom was one of my greatest role models.

For my father and me, it was a much different story. We never had a very close and personal relationship. There was never any real affection between us that I can remember, even going back to my earliest childhood. He was a good provider and taught us many things: right from wrong, telling the truth, being courteous and friendly to others, looking people in the eyes and using their names, a firm handshake, etc. He taught us well how to treat others outside of our home; we just never learned how to do it within our home.

After my parents were divorced, our relationship became more cordial, more formal. When I did see him, we said the proper 'hellos' and 'how are yous,' but we never went much deeper than that. A few verbal fights would flare up from time to time, but I moved out of the state when I was 20 and didn't see or talk to him a whole lot. He passed away a few years ago.

I remember going to see my father for the last time when he was in hospice in Florida. This was difficult... I had only seen or talked to my dad once in the past 20 years (memories can sometimes get in the way of moving forward). My son went with me and we were able to spend a few days sitting with my dad. Sometimes, we would reminisce, but mostly I would just sit near him, in his hospice bed, holding his hand on occasion.

One of the hardest parts of the trip was watching the clock on our last day there, knowing that I had to leave at a certain time in order to make our flight home. My heart was pounding, as I wasn't sure what to do or how to say goodbye. With about 20 minutes to go before I had to leave, God took care of the situation for me.

I completely broke down—just started sobbing uncontrollably—in front of my sisters, my dad's wife, my son. It took a few minutes to calm down a bit and gain some composure. I asked my dad if I could pray for him (something that had never happened in his lifetime), and he said, "of course." As tears were rolling down his cheeks, I asked God to bless this man and to bring him home.

I gave him one last embrace, and, as we got up to leave, one more endearing memory was made for me. My 28-year-old son, John Shay, who didn't know his grandfather that well but loved him none the less, bent over my dad, gave him a long embrace, and said, "Grandpa, I want you to know that you did a good job raising your son. He is a good man and a good father." My dad looked up at me and said, "I know he is." Those are the last words that I ever heard my father say. I will have that memory for the rest of my life.

Our lives are made up of memories, of experiences—all the things that have happened to us from the time we are born until this very moment. We are a culmination of everything from then until now. We don't choose our parents. We don't choose our brothers and sisters. We don't choose the families that we are born into. God decides all of this for us and there is surely a reason. That reason is much too difficult for us to try and understand. All we can do is take those experiences and what we have learned over the years and try to be better people.

We don't need to be better than those before us, but rather, we can try to be better ourselves. Those before us had their own experiences and memories and people around them that shaped their lives. We cannot walk in their shoes. We have our own footsteps to follow. We can all sit back and talk about 'if I only had the chance to do it over again' how much better life would be. But we can't do that. Even if we could, how do we know that life would be that much better? We are in the place that we are at right now because that is exactly where we are supposed to be. God doesn't make mistakes.

***

When I was 20, I left Michigan for a two-week trip to Texas with my sister. I ended up staying for six years. Talk about experiences! I had plenty! It was 1980 and there was an oil boom going on. I landed a job with a small company that sold oil equipment throughout south Texas. The owners of the business were a couple of young guys in their mid-thirties. They were both named Bob. These guys were hard workers, great salesmen, and liked to have a lot of fun. They taught me plenty: how to work hard, how to sell, and how to have a lot of fun. Sometimes all three overlapped a little too much.

A lot happened in those six years—some good, some bad, and some that I am not very proud of. What I do know is that God led me there for a reason. It wasn't the two-week trip that I thought I was going on. It was six years of meeting new people, gaining new experiences, learning about business and how to deal with and get along with others. I was also led there for a much more important reason: to meet my wife, Janet.

I met Janet one day when I walked into one of our suppliers' offices. She had just started working there and we were introduced. I would see her when I stopped by that office from time to time, or we would speak on the phone when I needed to order equipment. It was a coincidence—a rather big coincidence, thank you God—that brought us closer together. It was New Year's Eve, 1981. I was going to a New Year's Eve party with my roommate and his girlfriend that another friend of ours was hosting in the apartment complex where we lived. There were probably ten couples there, and me. As the night wore on, I was speaking with this other couple I had just met, and, as we are talking, the woman mentions that her sister (who was home with her family) might know me. She gets her on the phone and lo and behold, it turns out to be Janet. Seeing how I was the only single guy at this party, and she was home with her family, I invited her to come on over. She jumped at the chance (I actually seem to remember that it took a lot of convincing on my part)!

Janet came over and we stayed up talking until 5:00 or 6:00 in the morning. From that day forward, we were inseparable. We ended up getting engaged that March and we married in October. I guess that's what they call a whirlwind romance. Our son was born in January 1984 and our daughter in November 1985. For some reason, around that time, I was getting the itch to move back to Michigan. I don't know exactly what it was. I often tell people that it was the change of seasons that I missed, or that I didn't like the Texas heat, or that all my in-laws lived there (just kidding). But, in reality, it was God moving me along on my journey. We made the move to Michigan in 1986 and I went to work in the mortgage industry for a small company that my brother and his wife had started a year or two before.

I knew nothing about mortgage origination at the time, but had to learn quickly. I had a wife and two kids to provide for and plenty of bills to pay. Hard work was not a problem for me and I was always a competitive kind of guy. I wanted to become the number one originator in the company, and so I set my sights on doing just that. Within a couple of years I was there, competing every month for the top spot and being there more often than not.

We had our own home now and our debts were paid off. I was increasing my business every year and life was looking pretty good. I ended up starting my own mortgage company, and within a couple of years bought my brother's company and merged the two groups together. Janet and I built a large new home in a very nice neighborhood and I continued to work hard and grow the business. In 1998 I had the opportunity to merge my mortgage business with a fairly new financial service company with about 100 employees. I did this and became a shareholder in this new venture.

Again, life was looking and feeling pretty good; nice home, nice cars, great vacations. The company was growing at a steady pace and I was able to help build one of the largest practices within the organization. My competitive nature was in full swing and I was fortunate enough to be able to partner with one of the top advisers in the firm. I would go out and find the clients and she would provide the financial advice needed to take care of their particular situations. My partner and I worked together for about seven years, and then I stepped away from that practice to help start another group within the firm.

***

I was with this company for about 13 years when I made the decision to leave at the end of 2010. My decision to leave came at one very specific moment and I can remember the circumstances to this day. I was in a meeting with the partners of the group practice that I was helping to build at the time. I had worked with them for almost a year—the practice was growing, we were bringing on new clients—things were moving along as we had hoped for. The meeting was a review of what we had accomplished and what our plans were for moving forward.

Part of the discussion involved reviewing the compensation package that we had talked about when I joined the group a year before. When this topic came up, I can remember the reaction on the two partners' faces. Their reaction told me instantly that what we had talked about the previous year was not going to happen. I had this sinking feeling in my stomach that you get when you realize the wool has just been pulled over your eyes. In that very moment, at that very instant, I made the decision to leave the company.

I was brought up to believe that a handshake was as good as your word. I still believe that to this day. What I have come to learn through experience and dealing with others over the years is that that is not the case with a lot of other people. I wish that it was, but it is not. This was, and continues to be, disappointing to me. My father and I may have had our issues and I wish that we could have had more of a relationship, but he did do a lot of things right. Teaching us right from wrong and how to treat others with respect were a few of the lessons I learned from him. A good handshake and giving someone your word—and sticking to it—was another.

I do believe that this was also God's way of letting me know that it was time to move on, going all the way back to that Saturday afternoon drive across I-696 and my spiritual awakening. I began looking at life differently. I began to consider what was important and what was not that important. What were the things that I had missed out on and what were the regrets that I had? Where was God leading me and what was He asking me to do? These were some of the questions that had been going through my head since 2008, and it became clear to me in that meeting that I needed to move on and do something different with my life.

As I mentioned before, I am a processor: it usually takes me a while to make a decision—especially a decision of that magnitude. The fact that I did make the decision to move on in an instant was a little out of character for me, and all the more reason I truly believe that God was moving me along. Now I just needed to go home and let Janet know the good news.

Her immediate response was, "What?! Excuse me?! What are you talking about?!" Janet is not a processor. She says exactly what is on her mind the moment it hits her brain. She does not mince words and you always know exactly where she is coming from. Obviously, this was a little bit of a shock to her. She knew that my life was changing and that I was searching and asking God what He wanted me to do and where He wanted me to be, she just was hoping for a little more advance notice.

Imagine, then, her reaction when I mentioned that not only was I leaving this company and this career but that I was going to start shining shoes for a living. Janet speaks fluent Spanish and I love to hear her when she speaks the language, but I'm pretty sure there were some words that I had never heard before when she responded to the news about my new career choice (just kidding, of course).

Actually, after the initial reaction to my news, Janet was as supportive as ever. She has as strong a faith as anyone I have ever known, and she told me that she was behind me 100%. She knew that God would lead us, guide us, and protect us on this next journey.

My transition out of the financial firm that I had been a part of for 13 years was as smooth as I could have hoped for. The CEO of the company—a man I had known for over 21 years at this point and who is a brilliant business man—can be hard and demanding at times. I was concerned that we would not be able to come to terms on my leaving the firm and selling my shares back to the company. Any concerns that I had were for naught. He was as cordial and as fair as I could have imagined and he wished me nothing but the best for my new adventure. I will always be thankful to him for that and for all the knowledge that I was able to glean from him over those years.

Shining Shoes

"Though your beginning was insignificant, yet your end will increase greatly."

Job 8:7

My last official day at the financial service firm was December 31st of 2010. I took the next couple of months to get ready for the shoe shining business. Our son-in-law, Mike, agreed to help me get all of this started. He wanted to leave the company that he was with and so we partnered up to get this off the ground. Mike is an extremely hard worker and a no-nonsense kind of guy. I could not have put this company together without his help.

The first thing we did was purchase a used shuttle bus. We took all of the seats out and had it outfitted with buffer machines, electrical access, a work bench, and shelving. We ordered business cards and marketing materials and nice bags to put the shoes in after they were shined. We started calling on companies to see if they were even interested in using our service (I probably should have thought to do this before I actually left my other career, but fortunately, most people were excited about the service).

We officially began shining shoes in April. The service was well-received from the start. People loved the idea of us coming to them to shine their shoes. They were also giving us the shoes that needed repairing. We would take the shoes to several different shoe cobblers in the area that could take care of fixing them, and then we would return them on our next visit. We ended up purchasing another truck a few months after we started and then buying a shoe repair store a few months after that. The first year was a whirlwind. This was something new and we were not prepared for all of the little things (and some big things, like a truck breaking down on the freeway) that could happen. We got through it okay and after we acquired the shoe repair store, our son, John Shay, came to work with us and started to learn the cobbler trade. Janet started working with us shortly after that and it soon became a little family business.

It usually takes three to five years to get a company off the ground and make some sort of a profit. The first couple of years we were continuing to grow and bring on more clients. We were trying to fine-tune the expenses, but by no means were we close to the profitability mark. None of us were making a lot of money (and some of us weren't making any), but we continued to move forward and fine-tune the operation. We always strived to offer the best possible service to our customers.

We are now coming up on our four-year anniversary and the business is still growing and getting stronger all the time.

This does not mean that it has been easy. It has not been easy. The work involves much more manual labor than what I was used to doing for the last 30 years. I guess it really does make more sense to work at manual labor when you're young and your body is in better shape, than to start when you are in your fifties. But who am I to argue with the direction that the Lord is pointing me in? One of the biggest changes in my life, since accepting Christ as my Lord and Savior, is knowing that He is always by my side. Always.

I can go through each day now knowing that the work I do has meaning, that there is a purpose to what I am doing, a reason. It doesn't mean that I still don't question God and ask Him to show me why it is I am doing what I am doing. But it is comforting to know that even if I don't hear the answers clearly, that I can continue to do the work knowing that He is always by my side.

People ask me all the time if I am glad that I made the move, if I would do it all over again if I had the chance. Do I wish I could have my old career back? I answer them all the same way. I am very glad that I made the move and of course there are things that I would do differently knowing what I know now and if there were such a thing as a do-over. But there are no do-overs. I firmly believe that God has me exactly where he wants me and that He has a reason and a purpose for everyone. That reason and that purpose are revealed to us all in different ways, and sometimes it is hard to see.

My purpose at this time is not about shining and fixing shoes for people, but about touching lives. I think He has always called me to do this, even before I knew Him so intimately. Why else would someone, who had been an introvert their whole life, have been drawn into the sales and marketing profession? A profession that spanned over 30 years of meeting new people, building relationships, delivering speeches to hundreds of clients, and making sure that customers were well taken care of? My actual, physical, day job may be to shine shoes, but my reason and purpose are to continue to take care of people—to touch them in a way that leaves a much longer impression than the polish on their shoes.

That's what I would like to share with you now: my reason and purpose for where I am today and how the good Lord worked through me over the last 30 years or so in my business career. The things that He showed me—often through others—that helped me be successful, not because of the job I had or the company that I was with, but successful in my ability to build relationships with other people. There are 10 key principles—or bits of wisdom, if you will—that were important to me, not only in my career, but also in building the relationships with those closest to me: my family and friends.

I believe that these ten bits of wisdom will be important to you as well, no matter what your job or career path is, no matter what your income level happens to be, no matter whether you are married or single, rich or poor, black or white, tall or short, or any other characteristic or type of box that we would like to put ourselves in. We can all use some wisdom from time to time.

My hope is that these ten bits of wisdom will be helpful to you and your walk through life. Read them, re-read them, think about them, and try to incorporate them into your everyday dealings with those around you, especially those closest to you.

Bit of Wisdom #1
Know Your Purpose

"For I know the plans I have for you, declares the Lord, plans to prosper you and not to harm you, plans to give you hope and a future."

Jeremiah 29:11

What is your purpose? Have you ever asked yourself that question? Have you ever really taken the time to think about it?

A lot of people think that their purpose is in their career, because that is what they do the better part of every day, and it really seems to define them. As a society, we like to compartmentalize—to identify with titles, to define others by what they do. But is this really what our purpose is?

I've been working full-time in the business of building relationships since I was 20 years old. Talking and writing about business-related topics is something that I've been doing for a long time now—over 30 years. I've often thought about what my purpose is, and have considered it quite seriously for the past seven years, since January 12th, 2008, to be exact. That, of course, is the day that I accepted Christ into my life and I have been thinking seriously about my purpose ever since.

I've been married to an exceptional woman for over 32 years. Was that my purpose? I helped raise two beautiful, responsible, gifted children. Was that my purpose? I had a successful 25-year-career in the financial services industry.

Ten Bits of Wisdom from the Shoe Shine Guy   John Early

Was that my purpose? I now shine shoes for a living. Is this my purpose?

I think that some of us may go through our entire lives continuing to seek and ask what our purpose is. Or worse yet, there are those of us who think that we know what our purpose is, only to find out at some point that we are completely wrong. God created us all to be different. We look different. We think different. We feel different. He gave us all different personalities and individual gifts that set us apart from one another.

I still don't know exactly what my purpose is at this time. I'm not sure that any of us can ever be exactly sure. I do know that God knows for sure and I trust that He is always nudging me in the right direction. I have to believe that my purpose is not about shining shoes. Maybe it's about the people that I come into contact with every day. Maybe it's about those interactions, about helping to put a smile on someone's face. Maybe it's all about making someone's day a little brighter. Maybe it's about helping someone through a situation that has absolutely nothing to do with shoes.

I ask myself quite often how it was that God took such a shy and introverted person and somehow directed him

52

into the world of sales and marketing. This I do know: As far back as I can remember I have had a fascination with people. People fascinate me. They always have. Ever since I was a kid, I have had an overly-abundant interest in other people. What do they do for a living? Where do they live? Where did they grow up? Married? Single? Kids? How many? How old? And on, and on, and on...

I don't know where this comes from. I am a true introvert by nature, which means that I would be perfectly okay being stranded on a deserted island by myself. I've taken the Briggs Meyer Personality tests (a few times) and it always comes out the same: Shy and introverted, doesn't like crowds, would rather be left alone. Career choice: sales!

My overactive interest or fascination with people used to bug my kids a little bit. Every time they would bring a new friend around, the questions would start coming: "So what do your parents do?" "Are you from around here?" "Any brothers and sisters?" And on, and on, and on...

If they started dating someone new, watch out! That's when the really good questions would start to come up. I have several nieces (they know who they are), who wouldn't bring new boyfriends around because they were afraid I would give them the third-degree.

I'm one of those guys who, when his wife makes him go to the mall with her, goes right to the seating area somewhere in the center of the mall and says, "I'll be right here when you're ready to go." If you've ever been to a mall, you know who I'm talking about. We're the guys who can sit there for hours and just watch the people go by, one after another, fascinated by each individual and wondering what each might be thinking about or what is happening in their own lives.

Is this all part of my purpose? Is this God's way of letting me know that even though my nature may be that of a shy, introverted individual, my purpose is to somehow be around and interact with the very thing that makes me uncomfortable: other people?

Rick Warren wrote an awesome book over 10 years ago called, *The Purpose Driven Life: What On Earth Am I Here For?* It was a New York Times bestselling book and sold over 32 million copies. It is a great book for helping you to understand what your purpose might be and why are you here in the first place. If you have not had the chance to read this book, I would highly recommend it to anyone who is searching for their real purpose in life.

In *The Purpose Driven Life*, Rick Warren says it this way:

> Life is a gift...
>
> Life is a test...
>
> Life is a temporary assignment.

I was watching a television show last year about the career of Reggie White, a Hall of Fame football player, who is regarded by most to be the best defensive tackle of all time. He passed away suddenly, several years ago, at a relatively young age. In an interview replayed on the show, White said this about his career: "If I'm only remembered in life as a football player, I haven't fulfilled my purpose." He obviously knew that there was more to life than just his job, his career.

I believe that there is more to all of our lives than just our jobs or careers. Don't get me wrong, our jobs and careers can be very important and can be a big part of our purpose. I just think that our purpose is something more than what we spend 8-10 hours of a day or 30-40 years of our lives doing. Remember, we only have so much time here on earth, and tomorrow is not promised to us. In James 4:14, it says, "Why, you do not even know what will happen tomorrow? What is your life? You are a mist that appears for a little while and then vanishes."

Back in February of 2013, my pastor was delivering a sermon and in it he quoted a verse from Acts 13:36. It referenced King David's life from the Old Testament. It says, "For when David had served God's purpose in his own generation, he fell asleep (he died)."

That really hit home with me. I hope that I am fulfilling the purpose that was intended for me... I do know that I continue to ask God to show me what that is. As my pastor had mentioned (and I agree with), I wouldn't mind those words from Acts being on my headstone when my time on earth is over:

"For when John had served God's purpose in his own generation, he fell asleep."

There is a plaque that hangs over my desk in my office that a very good friend of mine gave to me a couple of years ago, shortly after starting this new business. It is a verse from Colossians 3:23, that reads, "Whatever you do, work at it with all your heart, as working for the Lord, not for men." I try to keep this in mind every day as I go out to do my job of shining shoes for other people. I try to remember the why, what, and who I am doing all of this for. Is it for the paycheck? Is it for the new car or bigger house? Is it for the next vacation? Or is it for something much bigger and something much more fulfilling and purposeful? I think it is the latter.

I say this because I have had the big paychecks. I have had the bigger houses and the nice new cars. I have taken the vacations to Hawaii, Mexico, and the Dominican Republic, and flown on the private jets. I have golfed at the best golf courses and eaten at some of the finest restaurants. This was all nice and I don't feel guilty or have any regrets whatsoever about having or doing any of those things. I just realized they were not my purpose. Things cannot be your purpose.

Janet and I sit down every morning and read a devotional before we start our day. The book that we currently are reading from is called, *The One Year Walk with God* and was written by Chris Tiegreen. There are 365 devotional readings that cover all different topics and aspects of your life. One of my favorites, that really resonates with me, is titled, "Representing Jesus." It starts

out with the verse from Colossians 3:23, and goes on to
say:

> We see our lives in terms of activity and
> achievement. We interpret our success in terms of
> what we've accomplished. So it only makes sense
> that when we work, we define its quality by
> externals—what we've done, whom we've done it
> for, and what results it will have.
>
> God has His eye on other criteria. He sees our lives
> in terms of fruit, which may include activities and
> achievements but encompasses so much more. Fruit
> involves those qualities the Holy Spirit cultivates in
> us: love, joy, peace, patience, kindness, goodness,
> faithfulness, gentleness, and self-control (Galatians
> 5:22-23). So when God sees us at work, He is more
> interested in how the work is being done than what
> it accomplishes. He looks at motives and attitudes.
> Most of all, He looks to see if our motivation is
> derived from Him or if He is peripheral to what we
> do. And if He is peripheral, He is grieved.
> Ultimately, every inch of our lives is God's, even
> our work.

Martin Luther once said, "A dairy maid can milk cows
to the glory of God."

So I don't think that what we actually do to earn a living matters as much as why or how we do it. Whether you're the CEO of a major corporation or the guy shining the shoes of the CEO of a major corporation, how you do your job, and what the motivation is behind what you are doing, is equally important for either job.

Once I truly began to understand this concept of working as if working for the Lord and not just for the paycheck or for a pat on the back, my work became much more fulfilling and rewarding to me. I started to realize and see a little more clearly that my purpose can actually be a part of my work, a part of something that I spend the majority of my life doing—day in and day out, 40 or more hours a week—for the better part of my adult life.

Step back and take a look at your work. Think about not only what your job is but why and how you are going about your work. Think about the motivation behind what it is you do and the reasons you are doing it. Think about how your purpose might somehow be incorporated into your job and how God may have you exactly where you are supposed to be for a reason. Think about what that reason might possibly be.

Think of Jesus for a moment. Think of this son of God, who humbled Himself to come down from heaven for the redemption of our sins. He spent 33 years here on earth and never wavered from His purpose. He died on a cross for our sins, so that man could be reconciled back to God. No matter what He did or what came to Him throughout His life here on earth, His purpose was always the same: to go to the cross and bring glory to His father.

Therefore, think of Jesus and what He did for us when thinking about your purpose. If His whole purpose and reason for being here was to glorify God, then, perhaps, that should be our purpose as well. We are not asked, called, or expected to die on a cross for others. That was something that only He could do. But we can and should glorify God in everything that we do.

It doesn't matter what it is that we do for a living. We can be a financial consultant working with clients who have high-powered jobs and are worth millions of dollars, or as a shoe shine guy, shining shoes one pair at a time. God can and should be glorified in either of those situations, or in any other situation or occupation that we find ourselves in.

I mentioned at the beginning of this chapter that I have been married to Janet for over 32 years. Was that my purpose? I raised two wonderful children. Was that my purpose? I worked in the financial services industry for over 25 years and am now a shoe shine guy. Are either of these my purpose? I think now that they were all part of my purpose. I feel that God has a plan and a purpose for us throughout our lives and in everything that we do.

That doesn't mean that mistakes were not made. That doesn't mean that it was easy. Janet is wonderful and is one of the greatest inspirations in my life, but that doesn't mean that our 32 years of marriage were a walk in the park. We had plenty of issues, problems, and concerns along the way. We were in counseling on more than one occasion and came close to calling it quits several times. God became the biggest part of her life 12 years before He became the biggest part of mine. He redeemed us both. That all had to be part of my purpose.

My children are great kids and today we have an awesome relationship. That was not always the case. As I was climbing the corporate ladder and obtaining all of these great things for the family that I thought were good for everybody, they were growing up and I was missing most of it: a game here and there, a dance now and again, a project or two that I missed. It all added up over time and before I knew it, they were adults and on their own. We've had plenty of talks about that over the last few years. A lot of apologies were made and a lot of forgiveness was extended. They both had a relationship with God before I did, and I thank the Lord today for that, as they were also a big part of what I saw in Jesus. They had a better understanding of what grace and forgiveness were all about. God redeemed our family. That all had to be a part of my purpose.

There were people I wish I had not blown up at or had honored or been more respectful to. There were choices that I should have made and some that I should not have made. I was working for the wrong reasons and hence making a lot of the wrong decisions. God redeemed me in my work. That all had to be part of my purpose.

Remember, God doesn't make mistakes. Our lives are a culmination of all that has happened to us, from the time we were born to where we are at this very moment. There is a reason for everything and a purpose for us all. Think about your purpose. Pray about your purpose. Ask God to continue to reveal to you what that purpose is. Seek to know your purpose and in so doing, God will be glorified.

"The two most important days in your life are the day you were born and the day you find out why." -Mark Twain

Bit of Wisdom #2
Character

"Simply let your Yes be Yes, and your No, No; anything beyond this comes from the evil one."

Matthew 5:37

I think that character ranks very near the top—if not at the top—of the principles that one can adhere to, not only in your particular job or career, but in your everyday life as well. Character is all-encompassing. It permeates everything that we say and do. It is a direct reflection of who we are. It's tough to fool people about your character. You cannot hide forever what your true character is all about. But if we do have character flaws—which we all do in some way or another as none of us are perfect—they can be worked on and improved upon, to make us a closer semblance to who God had intended us to be.

The problem, though, with attaining something like character, is that you cannot just go out and buy it. There are some people who do try to buy it, but that of course goes against everything that character stands for. No, character, is something that is instilled in us over time. We are not born with it, but we learn it from those around us: our parents, our siblings, our friends and co-workers. We learn what it means to have character and what it means to not have it. There is something inside all of us that lets us know right from wrong and what it is to have good character and what it looks like to not have it. It would be awesome if they could teach classes in school about character, but they don't, or can't. We have to learn this one on our own, by experience, and by paying attention to the good people and the good things around us.

Character is built over time. For me, it started out at home at a very young age. Being brought up in a strict household with eight other siblings, you learn very quickly the basics of right and wrong. We didn't have any time-outs. Punishment was dealt with quickly and sometimes harshly. Most of the time it was left up to Dad to hand out the punishment, but on occasion—if what we did was bad enough and Dad wasn't around—Mom could just as easily take care of the situation.

Schools at that time handled teaching us right from wrong pretty much the same way: swift and sometimes harsh. I went to a Catholic school and I think the nuns had special training in how to use a ruler effectively. Getting a ruler cracked across your knuckles is somewhat painful, but it will make you sit up and pay attention for sure.

Hanging out, playing, and interacting with your siblings, friends, and schoolmates can also teach you a thing or two about character. We all have that internal voice in our head that lets us know who is playing fair and who is not, who is trying to pull a fast one over on us and who is really trying to be sincere. Sometimes we're fooled, but that is all part of the learning process.

As we grow older and get into the work environment, we start to learn character traits from the people we interact with at work. Again, we will see the good and the bad qualities in everyone, including ourselves. There are times throughout each day that decisions have to be made and they can be a direct reflection of our character. Sometimes we make the right ones and sometimes we don't.

That internal voice in our head is the same voice that let me know on more than one occasion that I wasn't being fair, that I was trying to pull a fast one over on someone, or wasn't living up to the character qualities that were instilled in me. God puts that voice there for a reason and we know it as our conscience. Sometimes we listen to it and sometimes we choose to ignore it. To have good character and to continue to work on having good character, we need to listen to that internal voice in our head. There were plenty of times when I didn't.

One time in particular that I remember to this day happened when I was in high school. I believe it was the end of my sophomore year and I got a job working at our school over the summer. It involved working with the crew that cleaned and polished all the floors in the school, so that they would be ready when the next school year started. Our school actually went from elementary all the way through high school, so there were a lot of floors to take care of and this kept me busy throughout the summer. They brought in an outside company to manage this job, so I worked for them and not the regular janitor at our school.

After this summer job was over, however, the school offered me the position of actually working with our school janitor and assisting him in his daily duties. I took the job and it ended up being more than a way for me to make some money, it became a character-building job for me. All I had known about the janitor, who I will call Andy, was that he had worked there for years and that he was someone to stay away from. He came across as crotchety and what we thought was a little mean. The kids in the school had a nickname for him—partly derived from there being a tunnel that led down to his office and work area. The nickname was "The Worm."

Everybody that I knew referred to him as "The Worm." If you saw him coming down the hall or walking across the parking lot, it would be, "There goes The Worm." We would not say this to his face, of course, but under our breath, which in itself tells you a lot about our character at the time. It was one of those things that I never really thought much of because it had always seemed to be that way. Andy was short in stature, but a powerful man. You could tell that he had worked hard all of his life and was tough as nails. He wore that tough-as-nails demeanor on the outside, and that is why we kids would stay away from him.

After school I would go down the tunnel and find Andy. He would tell me what needed to be done and I would get it taken care of and report back to him. I would only work a couple of hours every day and sometimes I would work at night if there was a basketball game going on. My job was to sweep the court off between quarters and to clean up after the game as well. This is when I began to understand a little bit about the character of Andy. I remember the first time I had to work a basketball game. It was between quarters and I was out sweeping the floor. I started to hear the calls from the stands: "Hey, there goes Little Worm," or "Hey, Little Worm, go back into your hole." I would just keep sweeping, maybe try to put a little grin on my face like this was just in fun. However, what I was feeling inside was not fun. It was demeaning and embarrassing. I knew these people. We went to school together. Some of them were my friends.

One time I can remember walking across the school parking lot with Andy and all of a sudden someone yells out of a second-story window, "There go The Worm and Little Worm! Go back down into your hole!" I felt completely embarrassed and furious at the same time. I didn't know what to say or do and it seemed like a long time passed but I'm sure it was only seconds. Andy spoke. He said something to me like, "Kid, don't listen to them, they don't know what they're talking about. Just some immature kids, that's all." I looked over at this guy as we continued to walk and immediately saw him as a person—another human being just trying to do the best he can in this world.

That night I asked my dad if he knew Andy and he did. They were in Knights of Columbus together—or some group like that. He told me that Andy was a great guy, a very good golfer, and that he had been in World War II. He was a tail gunner in bomber planes and had been hit with shrapnel on several occasions. He had a family with children and was an all-around good person. My relationship with Andy began to change from then on. We had a lot of long talks and I got to know him for who he really was.

You can never really walk in someone else's shoes. I really don't know what it would have been like to have Andy's life—to have grown up in the depression and to have fought in a war and been shot at while you're up in an airplane, pieces of metal hitting you all over. To come home from a war and raise a family while working hard every day at a job where people are calling you derogatory names. I don't know what it would have been like to have walked in Andy's shoes, but I do know this: that year that I was able to work with Andy, I learned a lot more than just building maintenance. I was able to learn a little bit more about what it means to be a man. I was able to get to know a man that had real character.

There are a lot of attributes associated with character. Two that I believe are integral are integrity and honor. Without having integrity and honor as part of your make up, it is tough to have sound character.

So how do we define integrity? How do we know if we have it? How do we know if we don't have it? Does it even matter?

I think it matters a great deal, especially now, today. The word seems to be used quite often. You see it in the mission statements of a lot of companies, both large and small. You hear the word 'integrity' used all the time by people who, for some reason, want to let you know that they have it, and will stand behind it (politicians immediately come to mind). But what does it mean?

It is defined this way: Integrity is the uncompromising adherence to a code of moral values and principles. It requires soundness of ethical strength. This is a summary of the Webster's Dictionary definition of integrity. Some synonyms related to integrity are: character, decency, goodness, honesty, morality, rightness, and virtue. Some antonyms are: badness, evil, immorality, iniquity, sin, villainy, and wickedness.

So how do you know if you have it or not? I think that if any of us were asked the question, "Do you have integrity?" we would answer, "Of course I do." I think that within us there are varying degrees of integrity. It might look different when dealing with our families (spouse or kids), than it does when dealing with our friends, or the people that we work with. But should it be different? Should we have a different standard of integrity based on who we are dealing with?

I don't think so. I think we should always strive for the utmost integrity, no matter what the situation. And this is not always easy to do. Not for me, and, I'm guessing, not for a lot of people. We're human; we sin and we let the world we live in get the better of us.

I think that because of the world that we live in, it would be a big plus to get a little more integrity into our lives. We can think about the word integrity, and pay more attention to what it actually means. Maybe we can take a few more moments and ask the question, "What would Jesus do?" This is the man who set the standard for integrity (along with every other good and decent human quality).

In Luke 16:10, it says, "Whoever can be trusted with very little can also be trusted with much, and whoever is dishonest with very little will also be dishonest with much." Integrity is not just about the big things, it is about the little things as well. It is about everything.

When it comes to integrity in business or our work—which is where we spend most of our waking hours—Peter Drucker, in his book, *Management: Tasks, Responsibilities, Practices*, summarizes it pretty well. He says:

> The proof of the sincerity and seriousness of management is uncompromising emphasis on

integrity of character. For it is character through which leadership is exercised; it is character that sets the example and is imitated. Character is not something one can fool people about. The people with whom a person works... know in a few weeks whether he or she has integrity or not. They may forgive a person for a great deal: incompetence, ignorance, insecurity, or bad manners. But they will not forgive a lack of integrity in that person.

Oprah Winfrey said it like this: "Real integrity is doing the right thing, knowing that nobody's going to know whether you did it or not."

Jesus talked about this quite a bit in His Sermon on the Mount and, in Matthew 6:3, He says, "But when you give to the needy, do not let your left hand know what your right hand is doing, so that your giving may be in secret. Then your Father, who sees what is done in secret, will reward you."

I was shining shoes just a couple of months ago and I pulled a pair of shoes out of a bag that a customer had left for me to take care of. As I was getting ready to shine the shoes, I reached in with my hand to get a hold of the shoe and felt something on the inside. I pulled that something out and it was five $100 dollar bills. My first thought was *Wow, what a nice tip!* But obviously, I realized that this was part of his rainy day fund and he had forgotten about it. He never would have missed that money. He never would have known that it was gone. I could have just as easily put that money into my pocket and been on my way, no one the wiser—except for Him. He is always the wiser. He always knows exactly what is going on in our hearts and in our minds. That is what integrity is all about: knowing that doing the right thing is not always easy or comfortable, but that it is the right thing to do.

What about honor? Where does honor fit into our character? Honor is about your good name. It is about respect and dignity. Honor is about doing the right thing and living up to a certain code of conduct and having a reputation for doing what is right. Honor and integrity go hand in hand and are crucial to building our character. There are many people throughout history who hold a place of honor.

I've always been interested in history—the history of my family, our country, the world. It was one of my favorite classes in school. I didn't do so well in the math or sciences, but did okay in history. I used to like to sit and listen to my grandmother talk about her younger years. She was born in 1899 and had some fascinating stories about her childhood, her relatives, and what it was like growing up in a different era.

I've read quite a few books on history—many about the Civil War—including different biographies on Abraham Lincoln, Ulysses Grant, and Robert E. Lee, three very different men from varying backgrounds who converged at the same time in history to reshape our country.

I've read quite a bit about the Revolutionary War as well, about men like George Washington, Ben Franklin, Thomas Jefferson, and John Adams. I've read about Genghis Khan, Attila the Hun, and Alexander the Great. I've read about the Egyptian, Greek, and Roman empires. I've read *The Art of War* several times, which was thought to have been written around 500 B.C. by the Chinese military strategist, Sun Tzu.

We can learn a lot about the different people in history who had a part in shaping the world that we live in. There were plenty of good and honorable people and plenty of bad and dishonorable people. Knowing about what happened 50 years ago, or 200 years ago, or 2000 years ago gives me a deeper sense of how I got to where I am today, and where it is that I should be going.

One of the groups of people that has intrigued me over the years is the Japanese Samurai warriors. What fascinate me are the history and the role of the Samurai warrior. The word 'samurai' was first referenced around the year 905 A.D. They were an elite fighting force for various rulers in and around Japan. Not only were they exceptional fighters and skilled in military tactics and weaponry, but they lived by a unique code called 'Bushido,' which means, 'the way of the warrior.' There were seven virtues of Bushido which were as important to them, if not more so, than their fighting skills. The seven virtues of the Bushido code were:

Rectitude: Conduct according to moral principles; strict honesty; uprightness of character.

Courage: The attitude of facing and dealing with anything recognized as dangerous, difficult, or painful, instead of withdrawing from it.

Benevolence: An inclination to do good; kindliness.

Respect: To feel or show honor or esteem for; to hold in high regard.

Honesty: The state or quality of being honest; being truthful, trustworthy, or upright. Sincerity, fairness, straightforwardness.

Honor: A keen sense of right and wrong; adherence to actions or principles considered right; integrity.

Loyalty: Quality, state, or instance of being loyal; faithfulness or faithful adherence to a person, government, cause, duty, etc...

People like the Samurai intrigue me. This is why I like history. This is why I like to learn about different people, cultures, and times in the past. I wish that I had more of the Bushido code in my life... at the very least it gives me something to strive for. Imagine if we all had a little more of this code. But we don't need to be Samurai warriors to have courage, or respect, or honesty, or any of the seven virtues by which they lived. We just need to be us.

There was a man who lived over 2000 years ago who had all of these virtues, and many more. He set the standard for what is right and decent—a standard for how we should live our lives and how we should treat others. He gave us the meaning of integrity, honor, and character and he lived it every day of His life.

I've worked a very long time now. Going back to when I was 12 with my first newspaper delivery route. That's 44 years and counting. A lot can happen in 44 years of working with and providing service to a lot of different people. My character was tested many times—not only in my working environment, but in my personal life as well. I didn't always pass the tests. There were certainly times when I fell way short of the mark, when I saw a shortcut or an easier way and took it. There were times when I took advantage of a situation or of another person. There were times when I justified certain things or actions and called it just getting ahead.

This is not an easy thing to acknowledge, but it's true. Having character 100 percent of the time is something to strive for but is not always easy to do, at least not for me. Mistakes are made, shortcuts are taken, and your character is compromised. We are all prone to missteps in our lives. We can all exaggerate the truth from time to time. We can all climb that corporate ladder a little too quickly and step on a few too many toes along the way in our careers.

But there is hope. There is grace. There is forgiveness and having the ability to be able to move forward and learn from not only those around us, but more importantly, from the One who showed us and taught us what having real character was all about: Jesus. He never wavered from character. He never wavered from decency, goodness, honesty, morality, and rightness, either. He was everything that character and virtue are supposed to be and more. To be more like Him is certainly something to strive for. That is what we are called to do—to be more like Him.

It gives me comfort to know that there was an example set for all of us to follow and that all we need to do is look to Him for that example. Character, like most other good and decent attributes, is not always easy to adhere to. We all go to work in some form or fashion every day, whether it is to a corporate office or a construction site, whether we're a salesman or a tradesman, or whether we're a stay-at-home mom or a shoe shine guy. What we do shouldn't matter as much as how we do it and the character, integrity, and honor that we bring to everything that we do.

"Your reputation and integrity are everything. Follow through on what you say you're going to do. Your credibility can only be built over time, and it is built from the history of your words and actions."
    - Maria Razumich-Zec

Bit of Wisdom #3
Attitude

"I waited patiently for the Lord; He turned to me and heard my cry. He lifted me out of the slimy pit, out of the mud and mire; He set my feet on a rock and gave me a firm place to stand."

Psalm 40:1-2

Attitude is not only important in our business and working lives, but it is important in everything that we do. Let me begin by painting a little picture for you.

Do you like peanut butter and jelly sandwiches? When was the last time that you had one? What kind of peanut butter? Smooth? Crunchy? Extra Crunchy? What kind of jelly? Or jam? Or preserves? How much of each? Do you use a lot of peanut butter and just a little jelly, or not so much peanut butter and gobs of jelly so that it oozes out? How do you spread it on the bread? Sort of in the middle, leaving uncovered areas on the bread? Or do you fill in every nook and cranny?

Are you starting to crave a PB&J right about now? I love peanut butter and jelly sandwiches (if you hadn't already figured that out). Ironically, I only rediscovered my love for them a few years back, during the last two years that I worked as a financial consultant. During that period, I probably ate a peanut butter and jelly sandwich just about every workday for lunch.

I prefer extra-crunchy peanut butter, strawberry rhubarb preserves, and very fresh whole-grain bread. I used to make my own PB&J every night before I went to bed. It was one of the last things that I would do before turning in.

Sometimes my kids would watch me put this masterpiece together (again, they think that I can be a little quirky sometimes). And our dog, Scout, would always watch. On occasion, I would give her a finger-full of peanut butter and watch her try to get it off the roof of her mouth. I found it quite amusing, even though Janet would get slightly irritated with me.

Anyway, I put gobs of both the peanut butter and the strawberry rhubarb preserves on my sandwich. Every bit of the bread needs to be covered, and then some. When I'm done making it I actually lift it several times to make sure that it has good weight. That is crucial. It needs to be a weighty sandwich for me to fully enjoy it. One thing I don't like is any kind of a sandwich with very little of the good stuff between the bread.

Have you ever heard the phrase, "comfort food?" I consider my PB&Js my comfort food. I would actually get a really good, warm, happy feeling right around lunchtime at the office. I would put aside whatever it was that I was working on, clear a space on my desk, get out some reading material, and place it on the desk in front of me (but far enough forward so that I would have room for my sandwich). Then I would get up, close my door, and walk over to my credenza where my PB&J had been sitting all morning, just staring at me. Is this routine sounding at all familiar to anyone else?

I would pick it up, moving my wrist up and down to make sure the weight was still good, which it always was (it's not really possible for any of the peanut butter and jelly to escape during the day), and place the cellophane-wrapped sandwich right in the center of my desk. Then, I would sit down and proceed to carefully unwrap this delicacy. Are you starting to get a picture of this? Are you getting hungry? Can you imagine that first bite? And are you starting to understand how some people might think that I could be just a little bit anal-retentive?

THIS IS WHAT ATTITUDE IS ALL ABOUT!!!
Attitude is about approaching everything that we do in our lives with a positive outlook. Not just the obvious things—like our jobs and careers, where we're expected to show up with a positive attitude—but with our families and friends as well, and the people that we meet on the streets. We can have a positive outlook with all the mundane things that we do every day, like making peanut butter and jelly sandwiches. We are in control of our attitudes. We get to decide how we are going to act in front of others and when we are in different and/or difficult situations. Our attitudes are a reflection of who we are.

Life is good! No matter how my day starts, how it ends, or what happens in between, life is good. I don't mean this in some Pollyanna way. I certainly have my moments (a few of which occur on a daily basis). But as I sit here, deep in thought, I can't help but think of how truly blessed I am and how truly good life is.

There are certain things that I believe are crucial for having a good life, some of which I have already touched on. Things like integrity, knowing your purpose, honor, and character. And then, there is attitude.

Attitude can work for us, or it can work against us. Thomas Jefferson said:

"Nothing can stop the man with the right mental attitude from achieving his goal; nothing on earth can help the man with the wrong mental attitude."

It can work for us or it can work against us. It is part of the driving force which determines how our day, our year, and our life is going to go—no matter what our job is, or what our income happens to be, no matter the size of our home or our bank account, or if we're married or single, have kids or no kids, a college degree or not. Our attitude is key. One of the greatest attitude stories that I ever read was that of Victor Frankel.

Victor Frankel spent three years in a Nazi concentration camp. He was a doctor of neurology and psychology, and came to understand that in the horrendous atmosphere and condition of the camps, the only thing that the Nazis could not take from him was his attitude, or how he saw things, or how he responded to the situations around him.

He survived three years in the camps. His wife, his mother, and his brother did not. It is said that he was responsible for helping to save many lives during that terrible time because he was able to help show those around him how to change their attitudes as well.

After World War II, Victor Frankel went on to have a very distinguished career in neurology and psychology. He wrote several books and described his ordeal during his imprisonment in the concentration camps. One of his most famous quotes is:

"Everything can be taken from a man but the last of the human freedoms, the right to choose one's attitude in any given set of circumstances, the right to choose one's own way."

When I think about the Victor Frankels of the world, those who have gone through the unimaginable and have lived to tell the story, about how they used their attitude to get them through that situation, it makes me stop and take pause, and thank God that He gives us the ability to choose our attitude.

We all get to choose with every moment of every day what our attitude is going to be. We can choose to have a good attitude or we can choose to have a bad attitude. Or, we can choose to be indifferent (which comes across as a bad attitude). It is up to us to decide. No one else can decide for us what our attitude is going to be. Others can certainly make our lives less pleasant—or down-right miserable as in the case of Victor Frankel—but we still get to choose what our attitude is going to be.

I decided a very long time ago that having a positive attitude was much more rewarding, much more fulfilling, and much more beneficial to my general well-being. When you grow up in a household that is somewhat confining and constricting to your overall personal growth, (meaning you are unable to share any of your ideas or thoughts in an open forum—say, for example, around the kitchen table—for fear of some sort of reprisal), you learn very early on that you can look at the world in two different ways. The glass can be half empty or the glass can be half full. I learned to compensate for what was going on around me. Even if I didn't feel all that positive on the inside, I learned to be positive on the outside.

How exactly did this play out? Let me give you an example. There was an incident a long time ago that I remember with complete clarity to this day. It was a summer day. My best friend was over at our house and we were playing basketball in our driveway. We were probably about 14 years old, getting ready to enter the 9th or 10th grade. So this would have been around 1974 (obviously the incident has stayed with me much more than the actual dates). I decided to go into the house to get us something to drink.

When I walked in the back door I saw that my sister was on the family phone. For anyone reading this who is younger than 30 or 35 years old, the family phone was the only phone. There were no cell phones in 1974 and the phone was not push-button. It was one of those phones you may have only seen in museums. It had a round rotary dial and you dialed one number at a time. The phone was mounted to the wall in our kitchen and there were rules around using it. With 11 people in the house, Mom and Dad had priority and the kids were limited to the amount of time they could talk.

I do remember that this was a Saturday because Mom and Dad were out grocery shopping. I realized when I walked in that my sister was talking with a friend of hers who I also knew. I decided I wanted to get in on the conversation and started to playfully try to wrestle the phone from my sister. We were laughing and going back and forth trying to get the phone from each other when all of a sudden I saw the extreme look of fear on my sister's face. I immediately turned around and saw my dad standing there, just looking at us. I got a sick feeling in my stomach because I knew what was about to happen. My dad had bags of groceries under both arms. He casually set them down and walked right up to me, almost nose to nose.

He proceeded to do two things which seemed to last for an excruciatingly long time. He was yelling at the top of his lungs about how the phone was not a toy and how irresponsible I was for using it that way, and he was continuously slapping me across the face. One after another after another after another... After he was finished, I just stood there for a minute. A lot was going on in my head:

fear, humiliation, hatred, pain... I wasn't sure what to do and I still had one more little problem—my best friend was waiting for me outside, oblivious to what had just taken place.

This was by no means the right way to learn about a positive attitude. But sometimes life isn't fair and curve balls tend to come your way. You can either choose to give up and withdraw, or you can suck it up and try to move forward the best way that you can. I made the decision to move forward and make the best out of a somewhat bad situation. I walked back out to our driveway, and I can't remember exactly what I said to my buddy, but I'm sure it was something lighthearted and funny. Being the best friend that he was then—and still is to this day—I'm sure that he could tell by the deep red handprints on my face what had just transpired, but he never said a word. And as Forrest Gump so famously said once, "that's all I'm gonna say about that."

Fortunately for me, I found a way to cope in my early years; I became a dreamer. Your whole perspective on the world can become much brighter if you just learn to dream a little. Everybody is wired differently, and how your particular attitude style is programmed into your psyche is going to be different than anyone else's. Mine was fine-tuned and refined over the years by my ability to dream about things that could be possible. I have been a dreamer for as long as I can remember. My mom used to tell me, "Quit your daydreaming and go out and do something!" I was probably nine or ten years old at the time... and as I've mentioned, I was one of nine kids born in the span of ten years. Looking back, I can now certainly understand what she was doing—she was just trying to get us all out of the house.

My teachers handled it a little differently. Because of how much time I spent looking out the windows daydreaming (instead of paying attention to what was going on in the classroom), they rewarded me with the appropriate grades. I had plenty of C's for complacency, and more than my fair share of D's, which I'm sure stood for daydreaming. I guess I was pretty fortunate to have made it through high school. I must have thrown in just enough B's (Be careful or you'll do 12th grade all over again) to get the job done.

My daughter Jennifer and I like to talk about our high school days. They were remembered as good times for both of us. She loved being around all of her friends, the activities, and the social aspect of the whole thing. I liked it for a lot of the same reasons but also because when I was at school I was not at home.

Jennifer was a very good student. She took her studies seriously and graduated 120th out of a class of close to 1200 students. I never hesitate to remind her that I was in the top 100 of my class, probably somewhere right around 95th. She is extremely quick to remind me that there were only 105 students in my graduating class. *That's the power of positive thinking! That's looking at the glass half-full!* I don't say this to make light of school or of education. Janet and I stressed the importance of a good education with both of our children, and if I could ever get one of those do-overs, paying more attention to my studies would have been near the top of the list.

I still daydream. I think it has become a part of who I am. I think of things that might have been, and of all the things that still could be. The Shoe Shine Guys started out as a daydream, and I still dream of all the things that it might become.

Having a positive attitude is something that we have to desire from within. No one else can form or create our attitude for us. We can only do that for ourselves. There is currently—and there always has been and always will be—

a lot of bad stuff going on in this world around us. Some of that bad stuff can even hit very close to home. We can't control the attitudes of our families, our friends, our coworkers. Only they can do that. They are responsible for their actions and their attitudes, just as we are responsible for ours. We have to own what we do, our thoughts, our actions, and our attitudes.

My perception of my attitude, and how it manifested itself into a big part of who I am, changed a great deal after I accepted Christ into my life. I started to realize and to understand that the how and the why part of my positive attitude was developed and became a part of me for all the wrong reasons. I was using this upbeat and positive disposition as a mask, as a way to let everyone that I knew outside of my home—my friends, my classmates, the people that I worked with—see me as this positive guy who had it all together.

This façade never changed, even as I became older and moved away from home and started my own family. It never changed as I continued to climb that corporate ladder and become more successful in business, or when we moved into the bigger homes and bought the nicer cars and took the better vacations. I still always had that positive attitude going for me. To the outside world and to everyone outside of my home, I had it all. I had everything. Life was great.

But that was to the outside world. I soon realized after my conversion on the highway that none of that was real, and, worse yet, I had created the same type of household that I had grown up in. There wasn't the physical violence or the drinking, and I was never afraid to give my kids a kiss or a hug, but there was still plenty of condescension, condemnation, and outright negative nagging on my part. I could spend a full day at the office making deals happen and being productive, and was always quick with a joke or funny line to lighten the mood, but when I walked into our home, that was not always the case.

I was hard on my family. I was harder on the very people who I loved more than anyone else in the whole world—my wife and my two children—than on those that I had no real relationship with, even strangers. The shame and the guilt of this still wells up inside of me to this very day, even as I write it down on these pages. I brought negativity into our household. The guy, who everyone on the outside saw as this positive, upbeat, got-it-all-going-for-him kind of guy, could bring misery into his own home.

There were the unending questions: What's for dinner? Why that? Why is the house a little messy? What did you do today? Did you do your homework? Are you sure you should be eating that? And on and on and on I would go. There were the looks of disapproval. There was the selfishness on my part of "Hey, I've had a long day and I'm going down the basement to watch a movie." This was all a reflection of the very home that I was brought up in. It was a make-believe world of everything looks and feels great on the outside of the house, but we have turmoil and turbulence going on inside.

Thank You, God, for showing up when you did. I say that a little lightheartedly and with all the dignity and respect that He deserves, for it wasn't Him who showed up. He has always been there. He was just waiting for me to show up and ask Him to be a part of my life. I thank Him every day for doing just that. I thank Him for grabbing ahold of me that one fine day and shaking my life down to its core; for breaking me and tearing me apart in so many ways and for showing me what real love is. I thank him for showing me what the meaning of grace and understanding and caring for others is really all about. I thank him for teaching me about forgiveness.

My father and I were never able to have the kind of relationship that was intended for a father and son to have. But I was able to forgive him. Through God's grace and understanding, I was able to let go of the hurts and the stress and the turmoil that were all a part of the relationship that we did have. I have also, through the grace of God, received the forgiveness of my wife and children. We, as a family, have gone through a lot of healing over the last seven years or so. God has broken us down and brought us all much closer together. It was not easy and there were plenty of tears, but we continue to grow in our love and respect for one another.

My daughter, Jennifer, and I have always had a close relationship. We have similar personalities and have always just seemed to get along well. For my son, John Shay, and me, that was not always the case. We have very different personalities and that was not easy for me to deal with. I made his life more difficult by trying to force him to be more like me. All that did was drive us further apart. As he got older, our relationship was becoming more and more strained and we were heading down the path of my father and me. God has redeemed that relationship. It has not been easy. I don't think that any meaningful relationship is easy. But John Shay has forgiven me and we continue to work on and build our relationship. We are able to do this with God at our side. We pray together often, and as a man who was only able to do this one time with his own father, I thank the Lord every day for this gift.

I still have a positive attitude. I like that I have a positive attitude. I just now know that my attitude comes from a different place. It is not a mask that I put on to hide what is really going on inside of me and to let everybody on the outside think that everything is wonderful. My attitude now comes from the heart. It comes from knowing that no matter where I am, or what I am doing, or who I am with, that God is always right there with me. Always.

He lets me know that it is okay to cry, it is okay to be sad, it is okay that things will go wrong and will not always be rosy and peachy keen. He lets me know that I can be me. I don't have to put on a façade or a mask or put up the walls anymore. In Psalm 40:4, it says, "Blessed is the man who makes the Lord his trust." I am so glad that I have the Lord with me, that I can put my trust in Him. Knowing that He is always right there allows for the positive attitude in me to shine through.

Aleksandr Solzhenitsyn, the famous Russian writer who spent years in the brutal Gulag Archipelago (the infamous chain of Russian prison outposts where countless people lost their lives to hard labor), still had the attitude to say this: "A man is happy so long as he chooses to be happy."

Dale Carnegie said it like this: "It isn't what you have or who you are or where you are or what you are doing that makes you happy or unhappy. It is what you think about."

We all have free choice. God gives us that. Think about the choices you have when deciding about your attitude. You can either be positive or negative about your attitude and how you see the world. You can decide to be positive or negative with the people you work with, with your friends, or with your family and loved ones.

And one more thing: remember that what happens to us in our lives does not need to define us—try to have the right attitude for the right reason.

Bit of Wisdom #4
Goals

"I can do all things through Christ
who gives me strength."
Philippians 4:13

Far better to dare mighty things, to win glorious triumphs, even though checkered by failure, than to take rank with those poor spirits who neither enjoy much nor suffer much, because they live in the gray twilight that knows not victory, nor defeat.

- Theodore Roosevelt, 1899

Setting goals is important. Stepping outside of your box is important. What Teddy Roosevelt was talking about in this famous quote was that it is far better to go out and try something that is daring than it is to sit around doing nothing because you're afraid you might fail.

I've been thinking about writing a book for five or six years now. My wife and kids knew this, but nobody else. I was afraid: what if I wrote it and it wasn't any good? What if nobody liked what I had to say or they made fun of me for actually trying? What if it only sold three copies? What if, what if, what if... I realized that this was all just part of my own insecurities, my own hang ups, and my very great tendency to procrastinate. God always has a way of moving us all along in His own timing, and this was one of those times.

I started writing a blog a couple of years ago. I didn't think of it as a big deal at the time, but as a way to share with people some of my thoughts and experiences around my 30-year business career, and to stay in touch with and reach out to the people we were shining shoes for. It certainly started out that way. I talked about goals, teamwork, service, and trust, and topics that were generally geared towards business. I had a good response right from the beginning, and as I would see people while I was out on my shoe-shine route, they would comment on what I had written about and ask when the next blog was coming out.

I continued to send out a new blog every so often but found myself sharing more than just my business experience. I started getting a little more personal with my stories and was sharing my faith a little more often than not. I wasn't sure if this was the right thing to do because this was a business after all and a good number of the people getting the blog were my customers. I discussed this with Janet on several occasions. She, being the rock that she is, and always giving sound advice, told me to follow my heart. I did, and the response became even greater. People liked the fact that I was sharing not only personal stories, but that I was sharing my faith. There were, of course, some who didn't appreciate that as well. I had to be okay with that. I had to be okay that some people were unsubscribing from my blog posts. God directs us to be true to our faith and lets us know that it will not always be easy.

Over the last year or so, more and more people began asking me to write more and to put some of my thoughts into a book. Being the procrastinator that I am, I was still thinking about it when God, as always, helped make the decision for me. A couple of months ago I received a phone call from a book publisher who had gotten my name from a customer of mine that I shine shoes for. The customer had mentioned to this publisher that I was writing this blog and put her in touch with me, and as they say, the rest is history.

As I stated earlier, setting goals is important; this one just took me a little while to get to. For future reference, when setting goals, you should also attach an end date. I learned a very long time ago, as a 20-year-old kid from Michigan who happened to land a job down in south Texas selling oil equipment, that setting goals was pretty important. The two guys who gave me that first real full-time job taught me that setting goals was a way to measure one's progress, and that if you didn't have something to shoot for, some type of gauge, you really had no direction at all. You were like a ship without a rudder, just kind of floating along.

That was 30-something years ago, and since then I have read hundreds of books, gone to dozens of seminars, and taken countless classes, most of which were business-related. Throughout all of this, whether it was the books I've read, or the Dale Carnegie courses I've taken, or the Zig Ziglar or the Tony Robbins or the Tom Hopkins seminars that I attended, or any of the other educational classes that I took, setting goals was a common theme.

Jim Collins, one of my favorite business authors, co-authored the best-selling book, *Built to Last* in 1994. He followed that up in 2001 with another #1 best-seller, *Good To Great*. Collins allocates a good portion of each book to goal setting, and he doesn't just talk about any kind of goal, he calls them BHAGs: Big Hairy Audacious Goals.

All companies need to have goals. But according to Collins,

> there is a difference between merely having a goal and becoming committed to a huge, daunting challenge... A BHAG engages people - it reaches out and grabs them in the gut. A true BHAG is clear and compelling, and serves as a unifying focal point of effort - often creating immense team spirit. It has a clear finish line, so that the organization can know when it has achieved the goal; people like to shoot for finish lines.

I liked to set goals and I liked to set big ones. I wasn't always sure how I was going to get there but I liked to have something big to shoot for. I remember a company meeting that I was in that took place within a year or two of my joining the financial consulting firm. I was the outsider who had merged his mortgage company in with the rest of the firm. I started to bring a few clients into the firm that wanted to do financial planning and so I partnered up with a young adviser, who was an excellent financial planner—she just didn't have a lot of clients at the time. I figured I could help find the clients, and she could do the financial planning part. It made for a good partnership.

At this particular company meeting, our CEO was going over all of the numbers for the previous year. How much revenue did the company generate, who was the top performer—that sort of thing. The top performer had generated something like $700,000 in revenue, which was quite a bit at that point and garnered quite a lot of applause—even from me, although I still wasn't exactly sure how to put that into its proper context (I was still a little new to their type of business). Anyway, after the clapping stopped and our CEO took a pause, I raised my hand to ask a question. He very politely said, "Yes John, what's on your mind?" I asked him in all seriousness what he thought it would take for a practice to reach $1,000,000 in revenue. No sooner had the words finished rolling off my tongue than I could hear chuckling throughout the room from several people. I didn't know if they were chuckling because this was such a big number or if they were laughing because it was me, the newer guy at the firm who was asking the question.

In any case—and I remember his reaction clearly to this day—my boss, the CEO of the firm, and the guy who only a few years earlier had one giant BHAG and left a very lucrative job at one of the largest financial firms in the country to put this new start-up together, did not flinch . He didn't even acknowledge the chuckling that had taken place. He just continued to look me straight in the eye and said something to the effect of, "Absolutely it can be done, and there is no reason why it shouldn't be." That was all I needed to hear. Within a few years of that meeting my partner and I had built a $1,000,000 practice and grew it to well over $2,000,000 soon after that.

I started The Shoe Shine Guys in April of 2011 with one truck and one other employee. Our goal from the very beginning was to offer our clients outstanding customer service (and to make it to the end of the year!). We started with one client, then two, then three... and as word spread about our exceptional service, we grew. Today we have three vehicles, a full service cobbler store, and five employees. We do, of course, have other goals that pertain to revenue growth and quality and that sort of thing just as most other companies do, but our BHAG, our Big Hairy Audacious Goal, is still this: exceptional customer service.

When I began this new venture over four years ago, many people, including friends and family, have asked—and still do ask—the inevitable question: "Why step away from a successful 25-year career in the financial services industry to start a shoe shine company?"

There's not one easy or clear-cut answer to this question. For me, it was a gut feeling (or at least that's what I thought it was at the time), something deep that I couldn't quite put my finger on. As chance would have it, I was re-reading one of my favorite books a while back, Stephen Covey's, *The 7 Habits of Highly Effective People*, and was struck by the second habit: Begin with the end in mind. That end in mind is the very short story of the long road that led me to where I am today.

I first read Covey's book over 20 years ago, and it rings as true to me today as it did then. Covey's second habit, Begin with the end in mind, talks about envisioning what you want to see happen a year from now, five years from now, 25 years from now, and so on. He talks about lining up your daily decisions accordingly, whether it has to do with your work, family, faith, or any other areas of your life that are important to you.

As I re-read the principles around this habit, I realized that I started The Shoe Shine Guys for several reasons, the most important being my relationship with God. I wanted to create a company where how our employees, our customers, and even our vendors are treated is a reflection of my faith. So that at the end of every day, I can well answer the question, Did I treat people the way God wants them to be treated? I try to always think about a simple question that is written on the bracelet Janet wears on her wrist: "What would Jesus do?" and treat people accordingly.

I have set a lot of goals in my lifetime: little ones, big ones, and Big Hairy Audacious ones. How I now view goal-setting is different than what it used to be. When you have Christ in your life, how you look at the world and everything around you changes your perspective on goal-setting.

Paul said this in Philippians 3:12-14,

Not that I have already obtained all this, or have already been made perfect, but I press on to take hold of that for which Christ Jesus took hold for me. Brothers, I do not consider myself yet to have taken hold of it. But one thing I do: Forgetting what is behind and straining toward what is ahead, I press on toward the goal to win the prize for which God has called me heavenward in Christ Jesus.

Paul is saying that his goal is to know Christ and to be like Christ and to be everything that Christ has in mind for him. He had a past that he has let go, he is forgetting what is behind, and is moving forward. He is well-focused on his goal. I cannot dwell on my past or on the mistakes that were made from the time I was young until now. I have to be focused on my most important goal, to have a relationship with Christ Jesus, and through that goal will come a better relationship with my family, my friends, and the people I do business with.

Ken Hensley, a musician who played with the British band, Uriah Heep, said this, "I know why I am here and my only real focused goal is to live each day to the fullest and to try and honor God and be an encouragement to others. What the future holds is firmly in God's hands, and I am very happy about that."

Bit of Wisdom #5
Teamwork and Trust

"Trust in the Lord with all your heart and lean
not on your own understanding."

Proverbs 3:5

Teamwork and trust within a company are crucial, and yet a rare commodity within most organizations. Whether you work for a large company or a small firm, whether your team consists of one other person or several dozen, it is extremely important to understand what trust is and to be able to trust one another.

Not only is this difficult to achieve in the workplace, but difficult in our personal lives as well. I always thought that I had a pretty good grasp on teamwork, that I knew what it was to be a good teammate. I had grown up in a household with 11 people in it and there were rules and chores and certain things that we had to do working together as a team in order for them to get done (or so I thought).

I had played organized football starting in the 7th grade all the way through one year of college and thought that I was a good teammate (little did I know). I have been working steadily since I was 21 years old with several different successful companies and always thought that I was a valuable member of the team (not exactly). How did my perception of being a good teammate, and the actual reality of being a good teammate, get all twisted around? Easy: I didn't have the trust part.

In his book, *The Five Dysfunctions of a Team*, Patrick Lencioni says, "Trust lies at the heart of a functioning, cohesive team. Without it, teamwork is all but impossible." Building that trust is not always easy. All too often, we get in the way of ourselves. Our egos, our vanity, even our own personal agendas can get in the way of being able to open ourselves up to others. The challenge is to let down our walls and become just a little more vulnerable—to let people in.

My problem was that I had put up plenty of walls over my lifetime—all kinds of different walls—tall ones and short ones, thin ones and really thick ones, walls that had rows and rows of barbed wire on top so that absolutely no one could get to me. I was afraid to open up to anyone—to let people that I knew know what was really going on inside of me—even the people that I love the most: my wife, my children.

As a kid I didn't want people on the outside of our home to know what was happening on the inside of our home. I was embarrassed, I was afraid. I was ashamed of what others might think. I learned from an early age that what happens on the inside stays on the inside. It was nobody else's business. We were the perfect family that showed up at church on Sundays and looked as though everything was just great. This was how I learned to be a good teammate—I was able to participate and still keep all the personal stuff to myself. I was not going to be vulnerable. I was not going to let my walls down.

This façade—this fear of being vulnerable, these walls that I had put up—spilled over into adulthood and into our marriage. On the outside everything looked just fine; people thought we had the perfect life. But on the inside it was a different story—a completely different picture.

It's not an easy thing to try and always live on two different sides of the same wall. Let me tell you a story about how this living-on-both-sides-of-the-wall can play out and how dysfunctional it can all become:

I remember back about 27 years ago, when this young couple was expecting their third child. They were excited because they already had a boy and a girl and this was going to be the tie-breaker. They weren't going to be able to have any more children after this because going through the pregnancies was very hard on the woman and was taking a toll on her health. They were almost six months into the pregnancy and everything was moving along just fine. They were excited, people were excited for them, and they were filled with anticipation on the arrival of this new addition to their family.

The woman, along with her husband, had gone in for a routine sonogram to see how everything was progressing. The procedure went smoothly. They had done this before and it was always exciting to hear the heartbeat and realize that a new creation was growing inside and how wonderful this all was. The rest of the day went like any other day. The husband went off to work and she went back home to be with the other two kids. That night they received a phone call from the hospital, "Would the two of you mind coming by the hospital tomorrow to review the results of the sonogram?" Not a problem, they were new to the area and to this hospital; this must just be the hospital's particular protocol.

When the two of them arrived at the hospital and walked directly into the room that they were instructed to go to, life stopped for a moment. When they entered the room they were greeted by no fewer than eight different people. There were medical doctors, psychiatrists, counselors, and hospital administrators. All there just to discuss the sonogram! The wife broke down immediately. The husband continued to stand behind one of those walls that he had put up long ago. He was going to be the brave one, the strong one, the nothing-can-hurt-me one.

The people who were there tried to explain to this couple what was going on. The sonogram had revealed that the little boy she was carrying inside of her was anencephalic. Anencephaly is the absence of a major portion of the brain, skull, and scalp that occurs during embryonic development. There are only about 1000 of these types of cases per year, and theirs was one of them. The people in the room explained that if the pregnancy went the full nine months, the baby would not survive more than a couple of hours after birth. There was also a risk to the woman if she carried the child another three months.

They recommended that labor be induced as soon as possible, and to terminate the pregnancy. For a young couple this was a lot to take in. For a young couple trying to do life on their own with not a lot of history of emotional support, this was overwhelming. They did what the experts recommended and immediately checked into the hospital. The next morning, the procedure was started, and within an hour a little boy came forth. The nurse wrapped him up just like they would any other newborn and handed him to the father.

The problem with putting walls up all of your life is that walls do have a tendency to come crashing down from time to time. This was one of those times. As I held my son in my arms and looked at his beautiful face, I had no more walls at that moment to hide behind. I couldn't pretend to be strong for my wife or for me. I was broken and I was vulnerable. I was, at that very instant, what I was supposed to be: a real person. At this point in our marriage this was the most emotional I had ever been and the closest that I had ever felt to my wife, Janet. It was almost surreal that this was all happening to us and happening so fast.

And then it was over. And then the walls started going up again. And then everything on the outside looked as if all was okay and right with the world. What a fool I was. How misdirected and how misguided I was. How selfish I was. I sit here today, as I write this all down on paper, and wonder what exactly it was that God had in store for me through all of this. How could I go through something like this with the woman that I loved so much and within days of such a gut-wrenching experience start building those incomprehensible walls again? How could I allow myself to shut her out of my life emotionally when it was times like these that she needed me the most? She needed me to be vulnerable. She needed me to be part of her team, not part of everybody else's team. What did I do? I threw myself back into my work. I hit all the goals. I set all the records. I won the trip to Hawaii. I did everything but the one thing that I should have been doing: being there for my wife.

My walls again began to manifest themselves as not only my sense of humor, but also as my drive to be the best at whatever it was that I did. My sense of humor became the defensive mechanism that I used to divert attention away from anything or any situation that got a little too personal. My drive to be the best was my way of showing that I could be a good teammate; just give me the ball and let me run with it. All you had to do was let me know the rules of the game, what the parameters were, and what the previous high mark was for a certain goal or task, and I would make it my mission to break that mark or that record.

That works out really great if your sole purpose in life is to be a very successful businessman. If your one mission is to build the best company and not let anything else—or anyone else—get in your way or even matter as much to you. That was my life for a very long time and it became very easy to justify what I was doing. To tell myself that I was doing all of this for my family. I wanted to provide the best for them, the best home, the best trips, and the best life. I just wasn't providing the best me—not even close.

When God allowed me to fall off of my high horse on my road to Damascus, He not only opened up my eyes, but opened up my heart as well. I began to look at things and see things in a completely different light. He not only changed the way that I viewed teamwork, but more importantly, He started to work on me and my lifetime of trust issues. I had to rethink and reevaluate almost 49 years of how I viewed what it really meant to be a good teammate—not only at work and on the job, but at home and with my family as well.

When I started to think back over my career in the financial service industry, I had to face some hard realities. I was successful. I did help to build one of the largest—if not *the* largest—practices within the firm. I did bring in a lot of high net worth clients and develop a very successful seminar program within our group. I did this, and I did that, and I did a lot of things. The problem—and the hard reality that I had to face—was that this was all about me. I was doing all of this because it made me feel good. It was all about my pride and how good it felt to accomplish these things. As Patrick Lencioni explains in his book, I let my ego, my vanity and even my own personal agendas get in the way of being a good teammate.

It was even more of an eye-opener with my own family. I was telling myself for years that I was doing all of this for them—all the hard work, all the late nights, all of the trips and social events, all of the times that work came before my family—all so that they could be well provided for. I was only fooling myself. I was not providing the one thing that was of the most value to them: myself. Teamwork and trust is not just a catch phrase that we use in a business environment. Teamwork and trust is something that is actually more important for, and needs to be incorporated into, your family environment.

John Ortberg wrote a great book back in 2007 called, *When the Game Is Over, It All Goes Back In The Box*. This book helped change my life. I have given out close to a dozen copies of this book over the years to people I know and care about. In the book he equates life to a game of monopoly. We play the game to acquire as much as we can as fast as we can. Whoever has the most stuff at the end of the game wins. Here's the real kicker: when the game is over, like we do with all board games, we put all the pieces back in the box. All the houses, all the hotels, all the money—everything goes back in the box.

This is what life is all about. When this game is over, this game of life, it all goes back into the box. We can't take any of this stuff with us. Not our homes, not our money, nothing of earthly value can we take with us. It all stays here. This helped me to start looking at my life differently. It helped me to start prioritizing the 'whys' and 'what fors' of everything that I was doing.

I need to stop for a moment and be clear on this point: Because my priorities began to change and I began to understand what real teamwork and trust within my own family really meant and was supposed to look like, this did not make me regret the nice homes that we had built. This did not make me feel guilty about all of the nice cars we had purchased over the years or the beautiful vacations that we had taken. I did not feel guilty or bad about all the stuff that I had accumulated over the years. What I did regret, what I did feel bad about—and the reason that my sense of guilt was bubbling over—was at what personal cost and toll all of this took on my family.

When I accepted Christ into my life, and when I started to understand what it was that God had intended for me and how He truly wanted me to lead my life, I began to understand the value of having a real relationship with my wife and children. I saw their value, not the value of giving them something that I needed to write a check for. We are more of a team now than we have ever been.

I had to knock down a lot of my own walls first. I had to let my pride, my ego, and my vanity, go. I had to let go of—or at least diminish quite a bit—some of the defense mechanisms that I had incorporated into my psyche from my early years, especially my quick wit and my urge to lighten any uncomfortable moment with a joke or a bit of sarcasm. This does not mean that we have turned into the Cleavers, the all-American family; we are far from it.

What it does mean though, is that we are continuously and purposefully working on our family. We work on building the teamwork and trust among ourselves the way that God had intended it to be. We make it a point to get together every Monday night for a family meal. We ask each other about what is going on in each other's lives and we pray together. We are certainly becoming more vulnerable with one another, and this continues to make our relationships with each other all the more rewarding and fulfilling.

This is what real teamwork and trust is all about. Whether it is at your business or place of work, with your Girl Scout or Cub Scout troop, or with your very own family members, the willingness to let down the walls and be a little more vulnerable with those on your team is essential. God made us to be part of a team. He did not make us to be alone or to be lonely creatures—we created that all on our own. As soon as pride, vanity, and ego—and any of the other man-made attributes crept into our being— we started to separate ourselves from each other in varying degrees.

Start letting some of these negative attributes go—start thinking about the 'whys' and 'what fors' of what it is that you do. This does not mean that we have to give up our careers or the things that we have just to be a better team member. It just means that we can consider trusting each other more. It means that we should be willing to drop some of our walls and be a little more vulnerable with each other.

"Trust is the glue of life. It's the most essential ingredient in effective communication. It's the foundational principle that holds all relationships." - Stephen R. Covey

Bit of Wisdom #6
Respect

"Do to others as you would have them do to you."

Luke 6:31

I have included respect as one of the ten bits of wisdom because I think that, as a society, we are losing, or already have lost, some of what it means to truly have respect for one another. This is just as important in the business world as it is in our personal lives. How we treat other people is a direct reflection on ourselves. If we want to be respected, we need to respect others as well.

Albert Einstein once said, "I speak to everyone the same way, whether he is the garbage man or the president of the university."

A lot of us learned about respect from an early age—I know that I did, and it was usually about how to treat our elders. My parents used to say all the time: "Treat your elders with respect." This went back for probably thousands of years. The older people in most societies were revered and looked up to for the knowledge and wisdom that they could pass down to the next generation. They were worthy of respect.

Just think back to the past couple of generations. Think about how we viewed our parents and grandparents, and even our great grandparents. Think about the lives that they led and what they had to go through in order for us to be here. They went through World Wars and Great

Depressions. They may have endured uprooting and moving entire families from one town to another or from one country to another. They endured hardships that would be hard for us to even imagine.

I remember listening to my grandmother tell stories of when she was growing up. She was born in 1899 and lived on a small farm. She had two brothers and two sisters. I can remember her telling the story of the birth of her youngest sister. She was six or seven at the time, and she could still remember the screams coming from out of the barn as her mother was giving birth to her sister. She remembers the doctor coming into the house with the new baby, but her mom did not come in; she had died giving birth out in that barn.

She used to tell this story somewhat matter-of-factly. She didn't mention whether she had any regrets of not knowing her mother (although I would imagine she had some), or the fact that the family had to be split up and sent off to live with different relatives because her father could not raise all the kids and work. She didn't complain about only being able to go to school through the eighth grade, or about the flu epidemic of 1918 that killed over 20 million people. She didn't complain about going through the Great Depression, or about her sons going off to fight in World

War II. No, I don't remember my grandmother complaining about much in her life, and she lived through more than 98 years with all kinds of stuff going on. To her, this was just the way that things were.

In the dictionary, 'respect' means 'to hold someone in high regard or to show honor or esteem for.' This was how I viewed my grandmother. I always thought that not only was she one tough woman, but that she was one of the kindest and most loving people that I knew. I held her in very high regard and tried to always show her honor and high esteem. Looking back, I see where my own mother got a lot of her traits and characteristics from.

So what happened? Why does it seem as though we are losing some of that respect that we used to have for each other? Is it because life has gotten a little easier? Is it because we haven't had the great tragedies of years past or the hardships endured by our forefathers? Isn't that the way things are supposed to be? Don't we want better lives for our children and for their children to follow?

Of course we do! So why are we losing some of that respect, honor, and esteem that we used to have for each other?

Maybe it is because we have started to become a society that values our rights too much: I have the right to this or the right to that. I have the right to be right. I want what is owed me and I'm going to get it. I want what I am entitled to. This certainly has made life easier than what it was for our parents and grandparents, but at what cost?

I think what is being lost in this new age, in this ultra-modern world of speed, technology, and I-can-have-everything-right-now mentality, is the closeness and dependence that we used to have with each other—the real respect and sense of community that we used to have. We are starting to lose touch with each other as a community. When you start to lose touch with people, you start to lose the feelings of closeness, the feelings of truly caring for one another, the feelings of love and respect.

Jesus said this in Matthew 23:37-39, "Love the Lord your God with all your heart and with all your soul and with all your mind." This is the first and greatest commandment. And the second is similar to it: "Love your neighbor as yourself."

We are commanded to love our neighbors. And this does not literally mean just the people next door. It means all of our neighbors. The whole world. Everybody. This is the meaning of 'do unto others as you would have them do unto you.' This is why we are to treat others as we would like to be treated. This is what respect is all about.

How do we go about getting some respect back into our lives? For starters, I think it begins with some basics. Let's begin with some of the stuff that we were taught by our parents and grandparents. Let's be cordial with each other. Let's call each other by name. My name is John. Why would I tell you that? If you know me personally, or you have been reading my book up to this point, you know what my name is. So why am I telling you my name? I'm telling you because I think it's important to know someone's name—not only to know it, but to remember it and to use it.

Names have obviously been around for a very long time, probably since the beginning of time, and were just as important then as they are now. Most people like their name. It's important to them. It was given to them at birth, and they've been known by it ever since.

I was named after my maternal grandfather. I had never met him—he passed away a few years before I was born—but my parents wanted me to have his name. I'm not sure how they came up with all my other siblings' names:

Bill, Tom, Jeanne, Brigid, Amy, Paul, Anne, and Molly... I guess I never thought to ask. My oldest brother, Bill, was named after my dad, but I really have no idea about the rest.

Some people like to change their names. I don't know if it's because they don't like the name they were given at birth, or because they just want to be different. Professional football player, Chad Johnson, changed his name to "Ochocinco," which was his jersey number in Spanish. Eminem, the famous rapper, was born Marshall Bruce Mathers III. Kid Rock, the singer from Michigan, was originally known as Robert James "Bob" Ritchie. These guys all now use a name that has something to do with their professions. I'm not sure that would quite work for me. I wouldn't want people to start calling me "Kiwi" (a brand of shoe polish)!

There are also names that most everyone knows and that will be remembered for a long time, if not forever. George Washington, Abraham Lincoln, Martin Luther King, Jr., Gandhi. These people all had a lasting impact on history and the world, as did the man with the most recognized name in the world today: Jesus. Whether or not you believe in Him, most people know Him by name.

Our own names are important to us. We should recognize that, and recognize that everyone else's name is just as important to them, too. Dale Carnegie, in his book, *How to Win Friends and Influence People*, dedicates an entire chapter to the importance of knowing and using people's names. Says Carnegie:

> The average person is more interested in his or her own name than in all the other names on the earth put together. We should be aware of the magic contained in a name and realize that this single item is wholly and completely owned by the person with whom we are dealing, and nobody else. The name sets the individual apart: it makes him or her unique among all others.

Of his "6 Ways to Make People Like You," this is Principle #3: "Remember that a person's name is to that person the sweetest and most important sound in any language."

I try to use other people's names as much as I can. My dad taught me this from a very young age. "Look people in the eye and use their name as often as you can," he would tell me. I've tried to teach my kids the same thing. I sometimes slip up, forget a name, or worse, use the wrong name (yes, that can be embarrassing), but I still try to call people by name as much as I can. You see, it does make a difference. I can see it in their faces. It tells that person, yes, you matter to me. It tells the other person, I do respect you.

Another way that we can be teaching our children about respect and reinforcing it for ourselves is to treat people well in the workplace. We spend the better part of our day in a work environment, and how we treat our co-workers and our customers is a direct reflection on us. This does not always work both ways. Quite often we are not treated the way we should be, or the way we would like to be—but that is certainly not one of the commandments. Jesus did not say to treat others well ONLY if they treated you well. We are to treat others well regardless of how they treat us. Not an easy thing to do.

I see hundreds of people every day. I am in and out of all kinds of offices and buildings and different types of stores, and I get to see how people are at their workplace. Sometimes it is quite depressing. People can come across to me as if their workplace is the last place they would rather be. The service industry—which includes just about any type of company that exists today and has to at some point speak or interact with a customer—isn't what it used to be.

I won't use certain companies anymore or patronize particular restaurants because of the service. When I start to feel that they don't really care if they get my business or not, or if it's not important to them if I'm satisfied with what it is they are selling, then it's time for me to go somewhere else.

What is it that makes your company different from everybody else? What makes you different from everybody else? Whether you're in the automotive field, the legal profession, the financial services industry, the technology sector, or the shoe shine business, what makes your company different from every other company? I believe it is service—as simple as that. The one thing that will really differentiate one company from another, over time, is service.

Service used to be a pretty big deal, and was much more commonplace. As a teenager, I worked at a full service gas station (and yes, I'm dating myself). When cars pulled up, I would run out, start pumping their gas for them, wash the windshield, and offer to check the oil. Not too long before that, I could remember the milkman coming to our house. If you're a young person who has no idea about what I'm talking about, the milkman was the guy who would stop at your house every week delivering the milk.

In our case, he had to come by a couple of times a week—I had eight siblings, and we drank a lot of milk!

I can't quite remember when the gas stations all became self-serve, or the milkman stopped delivering, or diaper services went out of business, but it seems that over a period of time, we've become more of a self-serve society. I would also argue that, not coincidentally, we've become less social in that same time frame. The more self-serve services we have, means the less contact we have with other actual human beings. The more we do for ourselves, the less we interact with others.

I think this trend really needs to change, and I'd like to think it already is changing. I believe that service—truly good, genuinely thoughtful service—is important to most people. Little by little, most of us have become accustomed to getting poor service, or getting no service at all. And when we do get good service, it's like a breath of fresh air. A surprise. A gift.

Good service is a sign that you respect the person or people that you are performing the services for. It shows that you care about what it is that you are offering and about what it is that they are getting. When people tell me that they appreciate the job that we do and the quality of our work, it not only makes me feel good, but it also reinforces my belief that service—unexpected, exceptional service—really does matter to people. Service and respect go hand in hand. It is hard for me to imagine one without the other.

This doesn't mean that we haven't made our fair share of mistakes. We have. We started The Shoe Shine Guys with all the best intentions and with a goal to offer the best service possible, but that didn't always happen. Mistakes were made, slip-ups did occur, the ball was dropped. Where we grew the most through some of these mishaps was because of the willingness of some of our customers to come alongside us, like a real community should, and help us to learn and grow from our mistakes. That is, 'loving your neighbor.' That is respect. To those customers I say, 'thank you.'

Life on this planet seems to be getting more and more complicated all the time. Even though all the commercials and advertisements are telling us that they are trying to make our lives simpler, they are not. All we get are more and more gadgets and services that are meant to make us more and more self-sufficient. This, in turn, continues to drive us further apart from each other. We don't need each other as much anymore. Everything is becoming more about getting it faster and instant gratification. Real conversations with other people are happening less and less. This is diminishing not only our social interactions, but our respect for each other as well.

I had to change this trend in my own family. Our lives were all moving at breakneck speed and in different directions. It is very easy to get caught up in all of your own agendas and fail to see what is going on around you. Life seems good, and you look like you're happy. You have accumulated all the right stuff and you feel as though you are where you are supposed to be—but you're not. I was doing my thing, Janet was doing her thing, and my son and daughter were off doing their thing, and we were losing the respect and community that we once had for each other.

We decided about a year ago that it was time for us to get some of the community back that we once had. We all made the conscious decision to be intentional about coming back together as a family—a family that respects and loves one another. We now get together once a week for a family meal. We talk about what is going on in each other's lives and we listen to each other. This doesn't mean that we don't have disagreements or differences of opinion—we certainly do. What it has meant is that we have learned to respect each other's differences, and have been able to extend each other some grace (Bit of Wisdom #10).

So to all of you who are reading this right now, here is my challenge to you: Think about what community used to be, and what respect for each other used to look like. Think about what it means to call someone else by name or to give your customers exceptional service. Think about what it should feel like to do unto others as you would have them do unto you. And then go and do those things.

We cannot earn respect for ourselves if we don't first learn how to give respect to others.

Bit of Wisdom #7
Courage

"Be on your guard; stand firm in the faith;
be men of courage; be strong."
1 Corinthians 16:13

How does courage play into our lives? What does having courage have to do with our work? What does real courage even look like? These are questions that I have asked myself quite often over the last few years. Having gone back and taken a good look at my life before Christ, and then my life after Christ, has been a real eye-opener, to say the least. I am not a real emotional kind of guy, but looking back on what my life was, and how my life has been changed, has brought up all kinds of different emotions, and it has forced me to come to terms with the person that I used to be.

The person I used to be thought that he had a lot of courage, but he was wrong. What he did have was a lot of opinions, a lot of attitude (the wrong kind), a lot of quick wit, and facetious remarks. He had a lot of drawing a line in the sand and daring you to step on over. This wasn't courage at all, but the ability to be a grown-up bully—the ability to get the best of someone else because I had a quicker wit or could use bigger words. The ability to make fun of someone else because of how they looked or what they believed in. This was not courage, it was insecurity.

It goes back to what I learned as a child about putting up all of those walls. I didn't want to be the one to get hurt, so I learned how to strike first. And fast. And hard. It almost sounds like the perfect formula for a sound military strategy: Strike first, strike fast, and strike hard. The only problem with that particular strategy was that I was not in the military, and this life that I was leading was not part of any real, significant battle. My insecurities were not only a detriment to myself but even more so to those that I truly cared for.

The ability to have a quick wit when having a serious discussion with your wife is not a real benefit and is certainly not courageous. Using bigger words and being facetious with your children, is not a real good recipe for endearment, and is, by no means, courageous. Talking to your friends and the people you work with in such a way that you come across as, bigger and better than they are, only works to belittle them, and is far from being courageous.

One of the problems with trying to forget about the person that you used to be is that there are always plenty of people around who will remind you of exactly who it was that you were.

Here's one other example that I was just recently reminded of—of my trying to man up and look courageous. Janet was asked about 10 years ago to hold a Bible study in our home for women athletes from the University of Michigan. On any given Tuesday night back then, we might have between 15-25 women at our home seeking to learn more about Jesus. There were women from all different sports who attended. We had basketball and volleyball players. We had gymnasts and field hockey players. We had rowers and girls that ran track. I was okay with this, because they would all do this down in our basement and I could have my introverted alone time upstairs. Janet ended up mentoring quite a few of the women and is still good friends with some of them to this day.

One of those people is a good friend of ours who we first met 10 years ago at that Bible study. She reminded me just the other day about what a gem I used to be. She reminded me about how I would interact with them when she and a few of the other women would come over to our home so that they could have some more quality time with Janet. She reminded me about how I would start to question their faith and their own insecurities, and make light of the fact that these athletes, who all had their college tuition completely paid for, and seemed to have everything going for them, would need a crutch, like Jesus, to stand on. She reminded me about how I used to bring them to tears with all of my questions, facetious comments, and flippant remarks.

What a fool I was! These stories keep taking me back to the story of the Apostle Paul. How he was so passionate in his persecution of the Christians. How he was so righteous in his beliefs that what he was doing was courageous and the right thing to do. How he had to be knocked to the ground and stricken before he could really see the truth and what his real calling was.

What I have come to understand is that it was not me who was courageous, and brave, and someone standing by their principles: it was them. They were the courageous ones. They were standing by their principles and beliefs while being questioned and lambasted by someone who was doing it because he was uncomfortable with what they stood for.

There are two primary definitions for the word, 'courage,' in Webster's New World Dictionary. There is 1) the attitude of facing and dealing with anything recognized as dangerous, difficult, or painful, instead of withdrawing from it; quality of being fearless or brave; And 2) mind; purpose; spirit - the courage of one's convictions - the courage to do what one thinks is right.

When I think of the definition of courage, the first things that come to mind are our police force and our fire departments—the people who, by the very nature of their jobs, agree to put their lives on the line every day. They do this without question and more often than not putting the safety and well-being of others above their own. All you need to do is go back and look at the footage or read the stories of what occurred in this country on 9/11—of all the brave men and women who were running up the stairs as everyone else was running down the stairs. There are plenty of stories of civilians who did this as well—who refused to leave the buildings before their co-workers or employees were out safely.

The first definition also reminds me of all the people who are in the military today, or who have ever served in the military; that is courage. It is the willingness to sign up for something that, with one stroke of the pen, or with one official order, can send you into harm's way. Not everybody is tested with that kind of courage. Not everyone is called to be a policeman, or a fireman, or to be a member of our military forces. It takes a special kind of person and a special kind of commitment to follow that path.

The courage that everyone can have, and the courage that we should all strive for, is revealed in the second part of the definition for courage: 'the courage to do what one thinks is right.' I do, however, think that this definition needs to be changed a little bit. I believe that it should be changed to read: 'the courage to do what *is* right'. If we called it courage every time someone did something or stood for something that they thought was right, we would have a lot of courageous people doing a lot of the wrong things.

This world is filled with people who are convinced that they are doing the right thing and are serving a just cause. This has been going on since the beginning of time. This is why we have been given a moral compass, a conscience. We just need to decide for ourselves to use them.

You might think that that would be an obvious and easy thing to do, but it is not. It was not obvious and easy for me to do and my guess is that it is not easy for most people. We continue to get in the way of ourselves and let our own agendas rule the day. That is why it so important to get to know your purpose and to set some goals, to continually work on your character and your attitude and to build teamwork and trust with those around you. That is why it is so important to respect our fellow man.

Before I accepted Christ into my life, I was a man with very little direction and purpose. I thought I had it. I thought I was doing all the right things and that I stood for something. I could make a good argument, and I could state my case with the best of them. But I was misguided and misdirected. I was letting all of my own agendas—my personal wants and needs, my selfishness—get in the way of what were the right things to do.

My understanding of what courage means has changed dramatically since that Saturday drive in 2008. For me it is no longer about being the tough guy, or about being the strong one, or about being the person who will not back down in an argument. It's not about always being right, or being able to get the last word in. **Courage is about knowing what the right thing to do is, and doing it,** no matter what the world tells you it is. No matter what your co-workers tell you it is. And no matter what your friends or family tell you it is. Courage is about looking inside of ourselves, to that moral compass that we were all blessed with, and following our hearts.

Ronald Reagan once said, "There are no easy answers, but there are simple answers. We must have the courage to do what we know is morally right."

I had a tough conversation with my daughter, Jennifer, recently. I love my daughter very much and we have had a great relationship for as long as I can remember. She was always daddy's little girl and could get me to agree to just about anything with not only her persistence, but by her ability to smile and to give great hugs. Jennifer and I are alike in many ways, and although she has more of her mother's extroverted personality, and not my introverted nature, she is very adept at getting her point across, and usually coming out ahead in any argument. In other words, she inherited my stubborn, hard-headed, I'm-not-backing-down-at-any-cost nature.

I always thought that it was kind of nice that my daughter looked up to me. She was proud of all that I had done—not only in my career, but for all the things that I was able to provide for the family. She appreciated the beautiful home that she was able to grow up in, all of the nice trips that we took as a family, and for being able to attend four years of college and study abroad. She was so happy that she could have the fairytale wedding that she had always dreamed of. She was grateful, she was happy, she was proud of her dad.

The reason for the tough conversation: Jennifer was letting me know one evening about something that she and her husband, Mike,—our son-in-law—were thinking about doing. This was something significant in their lives and had to do with a rather large financial decision. She was running this by me, not only because I am her father, but because I have 25 years of experience in these types of financial decisions. As we were having this discussion, I found myself beating around the bush a little bit, while at the same time letting her know it was okay to move ahead with what it was they were thinking about. I didn't sleep well that night.

I lay awake, thinking about the past 30 years or so. Thinking about my little girl as she grew up and about all the nice things I was able to provide for her. What kept me tossing and turning and what I kept coming back to was the phrase "all the nice things I was able to provide for her." Almost everything that I had done for my daughter and for my family was about things. I was able to give them almost anything and everything that they could ask for or want, except for the one thing that meant the most to them: my time. I never really gave them much of me.

I had to reach down and find the courage to have the conversation with my daughter that I knew was the right thing to do. I had to let her know that not only did I love her, but that I loved our son-in-law and our grandson as well, and I wanted them to have a better life than the one I had provided for them. I had to let her know that it was okay to have nice things and to want the nicest things for those you love, but just to make sure that those nice things don't come at too high a price. I let her know that I paid way too high a price for most of the stuff that I provided for our family. Not in terms of dollar amounts, but in terms of lost quality time. I can never get any of that time back.

I know that my son-in-law, Mike, is a great husband to Jennifer, and a great father to our grandson, Lucian. I know that he is a good provider and would sacrifice anything to make them happy. What I thought about when Jennifer and I had that conversation is that their path was starting to look a little too much like the one I walked down 30 years ago. I didn't have the courage then or the wherewithal to get off of that path. I needed to let my daughter know that. I needed to remind her that she and her husband were better equipped than I was back then. They have God in their lives, which inherently means that they have all the courage they will ever need.

Courage is not easy. Doing the absolute right thing when you know it may not be the popular decision, or that you may be ridiculed by those around you, is never going to be easy. For most of my life I took the easier road, the more popular road, the less-ridiculed road. I thought that I had courage, but I didn't. What I did have was some kind of misdirected or misguided sense of what I thought courage was supposed to be: the tough guy, stubborn guy, mule-headed form of courage. And that is not courage at all.

I thank God every day for changing my life. I thank Him for my wife, and for my son, and for my daughter. I thank Him for my son-in-law and for our grandson. I thank Him for allowing us to stay together for all of these years in spite of myself and my lack of courage. I thank God for being by my side today and for giving me real courage to do what's right, not by the standards of this world anymore, but by His standards.

Philippians 2:20 – "I eagerly expect and hope that I will in no way be ashamed, but will have sufficient courage so that now as always Christ will be exalted in my body, whether by life or by death."

Bit of Wisdom #8
Regrets

"For godly grief produces a repentance that leads
to salvation without regret; whereas worldly
grief produces death."

2 Corinthians 7:10

The first seven bits of wisdom—Know Your Purpose, Character, Attitude, Goals, Teamwork and Trust, Respect, and Courage—are all characteristics or traits that become part of who we are. They are something to strive for, something to work on in ourselves, and to become better at. They are all attributes of a life centered on becoming better than not only who we were, but better than who we currently are.

This was a major transformation for me and for my relationship with other people—by other people I mean all of the other people that I ever had any kind of a relationship with: my wife, my children, my friends, the people that I used to work with, and the people I work with now. I had to scrap almost 50 years of bad habits. I had to take a really hard look at the person I had become, and throw out a lot of the garbage that I had accumulated over the years.

This was not an easy thing to do. A lot of us like to hold on to our garbage. I know that I did (and still do). We become comfortable with our garbage. It makes us feel good, and who wants to get rid of something that makes them feel good? When God got a hold of me and started to transform my life, He began to transform the person that I used to be into something completely different. This is not only a hard and difficult process, but a painful one as well.

These first seven bits of wisdom are about where we are now and about where we are going. They are about what we think about and how we learn to grow in our relationships with others. They are about understanding our past and knowing where we came from and what we learned along the journey. It's about taking that knowledge and understanding and growing in a positive way that is honoring to not only those around us, but, more importantly, to God.

The last three bits of wisdom—Regrets, Reconciliation, and Grace—are not only about where we are now, and where we are going, but they are also about where we have been. They are about redemption from the Lord for our past. They are about taking a look at our past and not running away from it. They are the three bits of wisdom that can help us to deal with the person that we used to be. It doesn't mean that we have to be okay with that person, but that we can come to accept who we were and be able to move forward from there.

When Paul said in Romans 12:2, "…not to conform any longer to the patterns of this world, but to transform ourselves by the renewing of our minds," he was giving us advice from his own first-hand experience. Here was a guy who was transformed by Christ, who did a full 180 and had his life completely turned around. He goes on to let us know that when we do this we will be able to truly see what God's will is for us, "His good, pleasing and perfect will."

When I was first transformed by the Holy Spirit, I had to take a long, hard look at who I really was and what my life was all about. I had to come to terms with the person that I was and how it was that I ended up in the place that I did. I had to review for myself the first seven bits of wisdom, and figure out what I needed to do to work on improving those seven characteristics in my life.

As I was working through that process and looking back on the first 50 years of my life, the word 'regret' kept popping into my head. I had regrets for all kinds of things. What I would have done differently, what I could have done differently, and what I should have done differently if I only had the chance. The problem is that we never actually do get the chance to go back and do things over again. Once the moment has passed, the moment has passed.

In John Ortberg's book, *When the Game is Over, It All Goes Back in the Box*, he states, "We need to ask ourselves what we are doing (or not doing) with our lives now that could lead to deep regret. Life always plays in a forward direction, it never goes backward. Once a move is made, there is no going back." In other words, I can't change what I did yesterday, or last year, or twenty years ago. But I can think about it, I can reflect on what I have or haven't done, and I can start to do something about it.

Regrets are a reminder of days gone by, of the things that we should have done, or of the things that we should not have done. I have no regrets for tomorrow; I have not been there yet. Ask me the day after tomorrow, and I may have a different answer.

I read a great book a few years ago called, *A Grace Disguised*. It was written by Jerry Sittser and is his personal journey through dealing with the tragic loss of his wife, his daughter, and his mother in a car accident. Jerry covers a wide range of emotions throughout the book including dealing with regrets. He says this:

> Regret is inescapable in a world of imperfection, failure, and loss. But can there also be redemption? Can a life gone wrong because of loss be made right again, however irreversible the loss itself? Can people with regrets be set free and transformed? I believe that there can be redemption, but only under one significant condition: people with regrets can be

redeemed, but they cannot reverse the loss that gave rise to the regrets. People can be changed by the unchangeable losses they experience. Thus, for redemption to occur, they must let go of the loss itself and embrace the good effects that the loss can have on their lives. They must somehow transcend what lies behind and reach forward to what lies ahead, directing their energies towards changes they can make now. In other words, they must seek personal transformation, which comes only through grace.

Jerry Sittser's emphasis in the book is dealing with the loss of part of his family and the emotions he goes through in working through that ordeal. When he talks about regrets, he is talking about the things he wishes he would have done differently, or had the chance to do over again, if those people were still with him. Loss of a loved one is often a tragic and emotional experience and can bring up many feelings of regret. But regrets can also harbor themselves in many other different ways and for many other different reasons.

As I was reviewing my life and going over the first seven bits of wisdom, I had to come to terms with all the regrets that I had: about my career, about the importance I put on my job and how I put it ahead of my family, about how I treated and interacted with some of the people I worked with, for my lack of appreciation and respect, for judging my co-workers unfairly, about my relationships with my parents and siblings, things I should have said or done while my parents were still alive, relationships that I should have worked on with my siblings, judgments that were unfair and/or certainly uncalled for, about my own family, the things that I missed out on because of my selfishness, my short temper and lack of patience with my children, and for the separate life that I led for so long away from Janet because of my drive to provide for the family.

Regrets do come in so many different sizes, shapes, and colors. We can become paralyzed by the number and the sheer size of them all. But there is redemption, there is relief, there is hope. In Jerry Sittser's book he goes on to say,

> We are forced to face the ugliness, selfishness, and meanness of our own lives. Then what? In this case, there are no second chances. We are left only with the bitter memory of our failures or even of the good intentions we had but failed to live up to. But God promises to forgive those of us who confess our failures, to absolve those of us who confess our

guilt, and to make right what we are sorry for doing wrong.

The gift of divine forgiveness will help us to forgive ourselves. Without it, regret becomes a form of self-punishment. We see the evil we have done and the pain we have inflicted on others. We feel an acute sense of guilt. We loathe our selfishness and foolishness. And we know that there is nothing we can do to reverse the consequences of our actions. Yet, a holy God imparts forgiveness if we sincerely ask for it; a just God shows us mercy and embraces us with love. If such a God can forgive us, then surely we can forgive ourselves. If such a God lavishes us with grace, then surely we can stop punishing ourselves and live in that grace. Divine forgiveness leads to self-forgiveness.

Forgiveness is an integral part in dealing with our regrets. We not only have to be able to forgive others, but maybe more importantly, we have to be able to accept the forgiveness of those we have wronged. Accepting forgiveness for the regrets we have had in the past is difficult because it starts with admitting you were wrong in the first place.

Admitting that I was wrong was a big hurdle for me to jump over. It was one of those very big walls that I had put up along the way and it took a lot for me to tear it down. I can remember clearly sitting down with my two adult children and asking for their forgiveness for the failures I had as a father. I can recall the discussions between Janet and me about my absence as a husband and how she extended me the grace and forgiveness that I needed in order to move on. Janet and I still have some of those discussions to this day. Admitting one's regrets and being forgiven is not about then throwing them in a drawer and forgetting they ever happened; it is about learning from the past and being able to then forge a better future—a better you.

Living a full life is a process. I didn't want to be pigeonholed into the same place that I had been stuck for almost 50 years. When God transformed my life, He opened up other doors for me. He made me realize that life is a work in progress and that moving forward is essential to that full and rewarding life. I am richer now than I have ever been. Not richer in terms of earthly wealth, but richer in terms of spiritual well-being; richer in terms of the relationships that I have with my wife and two children, my son-in-law and grandson, my friends, and the people I work with.

Regrets will still happen. I may do something today that I will regret tomorrow. But they don't have to define me anymore. I have learned to acknowledge them and to deal with them in a healthier way. There are some regrets that I can never take care of. I cannot spend more quality time with my mom or take back all the selfish things I did during her lifetime. I cannot build a relationship with my father now that he is gone. Only God can forgive me for the regrets I've had with the people who are no longer here, and I am grateful that He always does.

Bronnie Ware is an Australian nurse who spent several years working in palliative care, caring for patients in the last 12 weeks of their lives. She recorded their dying epiphanies in a blog called "Inspiration and Chai," which gathered so much attention that she put her observations into a book called, *The Top Five Regrets of the Dying*.

Ware writes of the phenomenal clarity of vision that people gain at the end of their lives, and how we might learn from their wisdom. "When questioned about any regrets they had or anything they would do differently," she says, "common themes surfaced again and again."

Here are the top five regrets of the dying, as witnessed by Ware:

1. I wish I'd had the courage to live a life true to myself, not the life others expected of me.

This was the most common regret of all. When people realize that their life is almost over and look back clearly on it, it is easy to see how many dreams have gone unfulfilled. Most people had not honored even a half of their dreams and had to die knowing that it was due to choices they had made, or not made. Health brings a freedom very few realize, until they no longer have it.

2. I wish I hadn't worked so hard.

This came from every male patient that I nursed. They missed their children's youth and their partner's companionship. Women also spoke of this regret, but as most were from an older generation, many of the female patients had not been breadwinners. All of the men I nursed deeply regretted spending so much of their lives on the treadmill of a work existence.

3. I wish I'd had the courage to express my feelings.

Many people suppressed their feelings in order to keep peace with others. As a result, they settled for a mediocre existence and never became who they were truly capable of becoming. Many developed illnesses relating to the bitterness and resentment they carried as a result.

4. I wish I had stayed in touch with my friends.

Often they would not truly realize the full benefits of old friends until their dying weeks and it was not always possible to track them down. Many had become so caught up in their own lives that they had let golden friendships slip by over the years. There were many deep regrets about not giving friendships the time and effort that they deserved. Everyone misses their friends when they are dying.

5. I wish that I had let myself be happier.

This is a surprisingly common one. Many did not realize until the end that happiness is a choice. They had stayed stuck in old patterns and habits. The so-called comfort of familiarity overflowed into their emotions, as well as their physical lives. Fear of change had them pretending to others, and to their selves, that they were content, when deep within, they longed to laugh properly and have silliness in their life again.

All five of these most common regrets ring true for me. I am glad that I now know that and am not figuring it out with just 12 weeks to live. The ironic thing about that statement is that I really don't know how many more weeks I have to live. None of us does. James 4:14 – "Why, you do not even know what will happen tomorrow. What is your life? You are a mist that appears for a little while and then vanishes."

There's a very famous song that was sung by Frank Sinatra called "My Way." It's about facing the end of your time and looking back on your life. I'm a Frank Sinatra music fan, but as I read the lyrics to this song, it made me really think about my past 56 years. The first two verses are:

And now, the end is near

And so I face the final curtain

My friend, I'll say it clear

I'll state my case, of which I'm certain
I've lived a life that's full

I traveled each and every highway

And more, much more than this, I did it my way.

Regrets, I've had a few

But then again, too few to mention

I did what I had to do
And saw it through without exception

I planned each chartered course, each careful step
along the byway

And more, much more than this, I did it my way.

The first 49 years of my life, I did try to do it my way.
And regrets... I had a bunch, but then again, way too many
to mention. I'm glad that now I'm trying to do life His way,
and not my way. I'm so much more at peace knowing that
someone infinitely greater than me is leading the way, and
all I have to do is follow.

Whether I live another 50 years or just another day, I know I'll have more regrets. I know that there will be things that I wish I had done differently. More 'I love yous' I could have said. More hugs I could have given. More smiles I could have shown. All I can do is keep praying, keep asking for His guidance, and keep trying to do it His way.

"At the end of your life you will NEVER regret not having passed one more test, not winning one more verdict, or not closing one more deal. You WILL regret time not spent with a husband, a friend, a child, or a parent."

- Barbara Bush

Bit of Wisdom #9
Reconciliation

"All this is from God, who reconciled us to himself through Christ and gave us the ministry of reconciliation."

2 Corinthians 6:18

Having chosen reconciliation as Bit of Wisdom #9 was a difficult decision for me. I was conflicted, uncertain, and a little confused as to the real meaning of the word. I spent countless hours talking with Janet about the subject, and as our discussions became a little heated, we found ourselves having to do a little reconciling ourselves. I read through several books that spoke in length about reconciliation and pored over the verses in the Bible that referenced the word. Still, it was a difficult task.

I decided I really needed to have it included as one of the ten bits of wisdom because without reconciliation, or the ability to reconcile, the other nine bits of wisdom could fall apart. Reconciliation is the ability to restore harmony in our lives. It is the ability to let go of anger, and bitterness, and resentment. Reconciliation is usually between two parties and has to involve forgiveness. Without forgiveness, there can be no reconciliation. This does not mean, however, that because we forgive someone there is automatically reconciliation. We can forgive others without being reconciled.

My father and I never reconciled with each other. I tried a few times over the years to reach out and try to create some kind of relationship between us, but it never worked out. What I did come to understand and to realize,

163

right before he passed away, was that I needed to forgive him, and to reconcile myself to what it was that we did have. When I decided to make the trip down to Florida to see my father a few weeks before he passed away, I had to do some reconciliation of my own.

I first had to forgive my dad. I had to come to terms with the fact that, as a father, he did the best that he knew how to do. As flawed as that may have been (and as flawed as it is for a lot of us trying to be dads), as mentally, and as emotionally—and sometimes as physically—painful as that was, I had to agree to suffer the loss of the childhood that I wish I would have had. I had to take all of that hurt that I had kept bottled up inside of me for so long to the foot of the cross and leave it there.

Those last couple of days that I was able to spend with my father were days of peace. I was not bitter, I was not angry; I had no resentment in my heart. I look back at those last few minutes that I had in his room and understand what God was doing. He was not only healing me and cleansing me of all the bad memories that I had in my relationship with my father, but he was allowing the two of us to come together for the briefest of moments as a father and son should—to be able to hold each other as a father and son, to be able to comfort each other as a father and son, and to be able to cry together as a father and son. These were moments that we had never before had with each other in our lifetime together.

Maybe I stand corrected. Maybe this was God reconciling the two of us even if it was for just the last ten minutes of our time together here on this earth.

Reconciliation is not an easy thing to do. It involves letting go of a lot of the stuff we like to hang on to, like our anger, our resentment, our bitterness—our feelings of having been wronged or abused. It means letting go of our right to be right. Oswald Chambers once said, "The hardest right to give up is the right to being right."

Our natural inclination is to want or demand justice or, worse yet, to seek vengeance. We often feel that we have a right to those feelings, and sometimes maybe we do have a right to them. It doesn't, however, mean that we should act on them.

Romans 12:18-19, says, "Do not repay anyone evil for evil. Be careful to do what is right in the eyes of everybody. If it is possible, as far as it depends on you, live at peace with everyone. Do not take revenge, my friends, but leave room for God's wrath, for it is written: 'It is mine to avenge; I will repay,' says the Lord."

One of the greatest examples of both forgiveness and reconciliation in the modern era was exemplified by Nelson Mandela of South Africa. In the foreword of the book, *Total Forgiveness*, by R.T. Kendall, Professor Washington A. J. Okumu says this:

> Nelson Mandela is perhaps the best example in the twentieth century of a man who has taught us how to forgive. After 27 years of political incarceration - the longest-serving political prisoner in the world at that time - he emerged unscathed and told his people to forgive their oppressors and focus on the future and on building a new, united nation. In spite of the devastating trauma of apartheid, Mandela chose the path of forgiveness and reconciliation rather than the policy of revenge and vindictiveness.

Archbishop Desmond Tutu, in his book, *No Future Without Forgiveness*, talks about the election of Nelson Mandela to the Presidency of South Africa in 1994 and talks about Inauguration Day on May 10 of that year. He states,

166

A poignant moment on that day was when Nelson Mandela arrived with his older daughter as his companion, and the various heads of the security forces, the police, and the correctional services strode to his car, saluted him, and then escorted him as the head of state. It was poignant because only a few years previously he had been their prisoner and would have been considered a terrorist to have been hunted down. What a metamorphosis, what an extraordinary turnaround. He invited his white jailer to attend his inauguration as an honored guest, the first of many gestures he would make in his spectacular way, showing his breathtaking magnanimity and willingness to forgive. He would be a potent agent for the reconciliation he would urge his compatriots to work for and which would form part of the Truth and Reconciliation Commission he was going to appoint to deal with our country's past. This man who had been vilified and hunted down as a dangerous fugitive and incarcerated for nearly three decades would soon be transformed into the embodiment of forgiveness and reconciliation.

Here was a man who had spent almost a third of his life in prison because he was speaking out against the apartheid in his country, who, more than likely, suffered many forms of physical as well as mental abuse during his incarceration. And one of the first things that he does upon his release from prison is to seek reconciliation with those in his country and who had put him there in the first place. I think what Nelson Mandela did was take all that had happened to him and laid it all at the foot of the cross. I think that he understood that only reconciliation between all the people in his country would bring the peace and stability that they needed to be able to move forward.

I think of how difficult this situation and ordeal must have been and then think about the times that I was unwilling to reconcile with someone because of a petty difference or disagreement; how I held on to a grudge because someone had rubbed me the wrong way, or I felt taken advantage of by someone I may have worked with. I've had to learn to let these feelings go, to give up the anger, or the resentment, or the bitterness. I had come to realize that not only was I hurting myself by hanging on to all of these feelings, but that I was hurting all those around me by projecting these hurtful feelings onto them as well. I had to quit living in the vengeance and justice realm and start living in the forgiveness and reconciliation realm. I had to quit thinking so much about what my rights were and start to understand what it was that God was asking me to do. Loving our neighbor (our fellow man) is not just a request from God, it is a commandment. We cannot do that well without forgiveness and reconciliation.

I wrote a blog post a couple of years ago (November 18, 2013) that I would like to share with you now. It involves reconciliation and has deep meaning in my life. Here is that post:

"I've been thinking quite a bit over the last couple of weeks about what I wanted to write about in my next blog. There are lots of different ideas and thoughts that will pop into my head as I'm going through my day. I've always got a lot of alone time on the truck while I'm shining shoes for people and this makes for good thinking time. I actually have people come up to me quite often now with their own suggestions on what I should write about. I don't mind this; it lets me know that more than one or two people are reading the blog.

As fate would have it (and if you know me at all by now you know I don't believe in fate, but that all things happen because of Him), I went to listen to a speaker the other night talk about leadership. It was a 45-minute talk in front of about 150-200 people. He talked about different types of leadership and different styles of leadership: a giving leader - Mother Theresa, a leader who takes - Osama Bin Laden, a peaceful leader - Martin Luther King, Jr., a brutal leader - Adolf Hitler. He talked about leaders who were admired and leaders who were despised. He talked about what kind of leaders we should be and that we are all leaders in one way or another.

We can lead at work. We can lead at home. We can lead our children, our friends, our peers. We have the opportunity to lead at any given moment. The question is, what will we do when that moment presents itself, and how will we lead? What will be our style or our type of leadership? Will we be admired or will we be despised?

It was a great talk on leadership, and I could tell by looking around the room that this speaker had the attention of all those in attendance. I could see that they were hanging on every word and that they were looking at this person as a leader. As I was watching this, tears were welling up in my eyes. I was getting all choked up. I was looking at the speaker and seeing the leader that this man was. I was, all of a sudden, not seeing the boy that I had known for 29 years, but the man that he had become. My son was the speaker and this was his first sermon in front of a large group of people.

At that moment, as a father, I could not have been proader of him. He was speaking from his heart to a group of teenagers who were craving leadership. My son, John Shay, is part of the youth ministry at our church, and his passion is helping high school kids find their way.

Part of John Shay's talk had to do with one of his favorite books: Herman Melville's *Moby Dick*. He talked about Captain Ahab's ongoing struggle with the mighty whale, Moby Dick. And as the leader of the many men aboard the ship, he led them away from their true calling and into tragedy and death. This story and what it represents means so much to John Shay and the struggles he went through as a young man, that he has a scene from Moby Dick tattooed on his upper arm.

People will ask him all the time, "What is the significance of the tattoo?" This gives him the opportunity to share his faith and to let people know, especially teenagers, that life can be tough and that there will be struggles, but if you keep your eyes on Him and continue moving forward, that all will be well.

Psalm 23:4 says, "Even though I walk through the valley of the shadow of death, I will fear no evil, for you are with me; your rod and your staff, they comfort me."

We all have a leader within ourselves. We can all lead in some way, shape, or form. Look for ways to lead. Start out small if you have to, but look. I saw a leader the other night who is touching lives and inspiring a lot of young people. He also touched and inspired one old man, and I love him dearly for that."

That was a very important night for not only my son, but for me as well. I was able to see him for the man of God that he had become and watch him do something that was having an impact on other people's lives. We were able to embrace afterwards and I was able to tell him how proud I was of him. John Shay and I were changing the generational pattern of what used to be the norm in my family's history. We were allowing ourselves to have feelings, to show emotion, and to show love to one another.

This was not always the case for the two of us. It was just a few years earlier that the two of us were heading down the path of the relationship that my father and I had. I had built up and hung on to a lot of anger, resentment, and bitterness that had become part of how we communicated with each other. I am not proud to say that John Shay also had a lot of these feelings, and that this was learned behavior that he picked up from watching me as he was growing up.

Our relationship had been fractured and continued to break apart from very early on. I was not the hands-on father that I should have been. I had a vision of what I wanted John Shay's life to look like and who I wanted him to be, but this was not the vision that he had for himself. I liked John Wayne movies and football. John Shay liked Star Wars and video games. I was not willing to take an interest in the things that he liked and cared about, and so ended up missing out on a lot of what was important to him as a child and as a young adult.

I thought that if I just was able to provide a nice home and great vacations and the finer things in life to my son, that this would be enough. I wasn't even close. My son has a deep heart and an emotional spirit, and things do not matter to him nearly as much as love, affection, and taking a genuine interest in him as a person does. I failed at all of these things in a big way. Once again I thank the Lord for knocking me down off of my high horse and for transforming my life.

John Shay and I were able to break this cycle but it was by no means an easy experience. It took a lot of time and a lot of trial and error. We had to get out a lot of the anger and resentment and bitterness that had built up in both of us over the years. This was not a pleasant experience and was downright ugly at times. I had to do and say some things that had never been part of my vernacular. I needed to let John Shay know that I did fail him as a father early on, and to sincerely ask him for his forgiveness. Because of the man that he had become, he was not only able to forgive me, but he was able to set the reconciliation process in motion. We ended up bringing in a third party to this process of reconciliation. Someone that we both respected and who knew both of us well enough to ask us the tough questions. This person helped tremendously and was able to lay down a good foundation and get us headed in the right direction.

We are now both on a much different path with each other that will not only strengthen the father/son relationship for years to come, but will break the pattern of unhealthiness that was part of my life for so long. The Lord has reconciled us to each other in ways that could not have been imagined just a few short years ago. We are now partners in The Shoe Shine Guys and work together every day. We share our ups and downs and are able to communicate and listen to each other with genuine concern. I am interested in who John Shay is and what it is that he likes to do. John Shay still doesn't care for John Wayne movies and I am still not a Star Wars fan, but at least now we respect that about each other.

Having an understanding of reconciliation and being able to reconcile with others is a key bit of wisdom to have in your arsenal. God calls us to do that for a reason. It can often be a painful process. It can be a humbling experience. But it can also be one of the most rewarding things that we can learn to do in life. God lets us know that some of the most painful experiences in life will end up being some of the most rewarding for us as well.

I am glad that I was able to learn about forgiveness and reconciliation even at this late stage in my life. I understand now that God allowed me to have those precious last few minutes with my father for a very specific reason. He was allowing the two of us to break that cycle of the non-emotional, non-affectionate, non-feeling patterns that had defined our relationship for all of our life together. He was allowing me the ability to move on and to create a relationship with my son, John Shay, one that would be redefined and strengthened for generations to come.

Booker T. Washington was able to take all of the anger, hatred, resentment, and bitterness that he had—and that people threw at him throughout his life—and lay it at the foot of the cross. He was quoted as saying, "I will not permit any man to narrow and degrade my soul by making

me hate him." He obviously had a firm grasp on what
forgiveness and reconciliation were.

Bit of Wisdom #10
Grace

"But he said to me, 'My grace is sufficient for you, for my power is made perfect in weakness.'"
2 Corinthians 12:9

Janet has taught a Bible study class out of our home for more than 16 years now. Hundreds of people have gone through the study—many of them more than once. Men and women of all ages have attended the study. Some have attended who were in their mid-to-late seventies, as well as the student athletes from the University of Michigan a few years back who were in their late teens to early twenties, and every age in between.

Janet will still get a card or a letter every so often from someone who attended long ago, maybe even 10-15 years ago. They will express their thankfulness and gratitude for what they learned and how the experience somehow changed their life.

The format or outline of the study is always the same. There are 23 different cards or topics, and she goes over a different one each week for 23 weeks. How Janet teaches each card every week, though, is never the same. I know this because for the last five years I have attended the study, and have never seen her teach the same card the same way.

My wife is an amazing person. I'm not saying this because she is my wife (although that never hurts). I'm saying it because I've been to a lot of seminars over the years, attended dozens of lectures and conferences, gone to quite a few classes, and met hundreds of professionals from all walks of life. No one has impacted me more from a human standpoint than my wife. And, as we are out and about—whether it be at church, or the mall, the grocery store or wherever—it usually never fails that we will run into someone who comes up to my wife, gives her a big hug, and starts thanking her for something she did for them.

What is this study that she teaches? It is a study about grace. It's about restoring grace into our lives. It's about accepting God's grace—which is never-ending—and being able to extend grace to others. This is not an easy thing to do. As humans we want to be in charge of our own lives. We want things to go our way. We don't especially like it when others don't go along with our plan.

Grace is mentioned over 50 times in the Bible. God promises us that His grace will never leave us. I like two definitions in the dictionary about grace. The human definition: 'a sense of what is right and proper; decency; thoughtfulness towards others.' And the theological definition: 'the unmerited love and favor of God toward man.' This second definition means that God always gives us His love and extends us His grace, even though we don't deserve it.

As hard as we would like to try, there are not enough good things that we could do here on this earth to earn God's grace. We cannot earn His grace; it is given to us as a gift. It is given freely to us all, we just have to be able to accept it. That's where things can get a little sticky. It is sometimes difficult to be able to see grace for the gift that it truly is, instead of thinking that you have go through life trying to earn it. I spent the better part of my life trying to do just that—to earn it.

When I was a younger man, I couldn't get the one person that I looked up to, to be proud of me—or at least acknowledge that he was proud of me—and this caused me to overcompensate. Somewhere along the line, I made the decision that I would succeed at whatever it was that I did. I would work to be the best at whatever endeavor I took on. I would make that person proud of me, no matter what it took. And it ended up taking a lot.

I went through life thinking that I was actually in charge of my life. I was a man's man. Give me a challenge and I will take it on. I wanted to be number one. And in a lot of ways I was. I was successful and got a lot of pats on the back. I was doing everything that you were supposed to do when you have a job, except that I was doing it all for the wrong reasons. And the kicker about all of this is that the person who was proudest of all was me. Pride had become my partner—my friend. I was living the definition of pride: 'a feeling of deep pleasure or satisfaction derived from one's own achievements, the achievements of those with whom one is closely associated, or from qualities or possessions that are widely admired.'

Charles Spurgeon, the famous nineteenth century English preacher, once said, "The greatest enemy to human souls is the self-righteous spirit which makes men look to themselves for salvation." I was looking to myself for not only salvation, but for everything. If it was going to happen, then I was the one who was going to make it happen.

Paul's second letter to the Corinthians, in Chapter 12, talks about some things that Paul had said that could be construed as prideful. Because of Paul's boastfulness, God had put a thorn in his side. This was some type of debilitating illness that kept Paul from his normal workload. Paul asked God on three separate occasions to remove this thorn, but He refused, saying in verse 9, "My grace is sufficient for you, for my power is made great in weakness."

I believe that God did the same thing for me after my transformation and let me know that grace—not pride—was the road that I needed to be on. I finally began to understand that I didn't have to continue trying so hard to get others to be proud of me. I could take my audience—this giant mass of people who I was looking to for acceptance—and bring it down to an audience of one. Knowing that Jesus Christ had given me this free gift of grace, forgiveness, and reconciliation, and that He was the ultimate Father, who had always been proud of not only me, but all of his children, was the truest bit of wisdom I needed to give me peace.

Grace was a difficult concept for me to fully grasp early on in my transformation, and I still struggle today with my pride and selfishness. I had very little—if any—grace in my life for the first 49 years of my existence. It was all about me. What could I get? What could I do? What could I become? I was living in a world that revolved around John Early, and almost every action that I took had to do with 'what's in it for me?'

Even when it came to those around me—my wife and children, especially—I was always pressing my wants and needs onto their lives. I wanted order in my life (my anal-retentiveness or OCD), and I expected that out of Janet and the kids. When I got home from work, the house needed to be cleaned and well-kept. The backpacks were not supposed to be sitting on the kitchen table. My questions would start popping up after I walked in: Did you do your homework? Are your rooms clean? What happened at practice today? Janet, what did you do all day? What's for dinner? *Zero Grace*!!

All of those great vacations that we took weren't that great when everything was all about me. I want to do this. I want to do that. I don't want to do anything but sit here and relax. This was *my* vacation by the way and I worked hard for this (as if Janet had nothing to do with any of this). Our big, beautiful home was awesome, *for me*! I provided this for my family and then proceeded to make home life almost unbearable by the amount of expectations I put on Janet to maintain and keep the place up. *Zero Grace*!!

Janet and I used to take turns every other year and plan something for our wedding anniversary. It was always a surprise for the other person, and our friends and family thought that this was so cool that we would do this for each other every year. Looking back, I realize that this was cool for me but was a stressful, painful, and sometimes hurtful situation for Janet. I would plan the extravagant trips and money was no object. But when it came time for her to plan the trip, I would usually make her feel guilty for how much it was all going to cost, or I would express that I hoped the place we were going was somewhere that I liked.

One year, maybe 15 years ago or so, it was Janet's turn to plan the trip. We were having some difficult times in our marriage (which was happening more often than not) and she wanted to plan something special. These trips were usually long weekends, and on occasion we would be able to drive to the specific location. This was one of those driving trips, and as we started out on a Friday afternoon, I was filled with anticipation.

We ended up driving about an hour west of the Detroit area when she instructed me to take the next exit for Lansing. We made a few more turns and then pulled into a nice hotel in the area. I was thinking, okay, this will be nice, just the two of us alone for the weekend. We checked in and got into the elevator to head up to our room. Everything good so far! And then it happened. There was another couple in the elevator, and within seconds of the door closing, the other woman says very enthusiastically, "So, you guys are here for the marriage conference, too, huh?"

My blood pressure immediately hit the roof. My eyes widened and my jaw must have dropped because the other gentleman in the elevator could tell right away that this was a surprise to me. He looked at his wife and said, "Really, honey? You just don't know when to keep your mouth shut, do you?" (By the look that she then gave him I could tell that they were there for some very specific reasons). The next hour or two were not some of my finest moments. When Janet and I got to our room I proceeded to let her have it with both barrels. It reminds me now of how I reacted towards my mom, back when I was a teenager and came into our house to find the Thanksgiving baskets for the needy on our kitchen table. *Zero Grace then, and Zero Grace now*!!

Janet and I ended up staying for the weekend but I remember that I was just going through the motions thinking, *What kind of a vacation is this?* After that episode I would use this situation and make facetious remarks to others from time to time about my "marriage conference vacation." I look back now and wonder how somebody could be so ignorant of others' feelings. How could I be so callous and have such a lack of compassion or understanding for another human being, let alone someone I loved so much? How could I put such pressure on my wife and children when they were doing nothing but looking to me for love and support? It amazes me to this day that God had kept us all together.

In Philippians 2:3, it says, "Do nothing out of selfish ambition or vain conceit, but in humility consider others better than yourselves."

It took God allowing me to be knocked off of my very high horse, and humbling me to my core, to make me realize the gifts that He had laid before me. I had the gift of Janet, who stood by me through thick and thin and never gave up on the two of us. A wife who prayed for 12 years that God would take hold of her husband's life just as He had taken hold of hers. A wife who has been my rock for over 33 years and continues to inspire me and walk beside me on this journey we call life.

I had the gift of two beautiful children, John Shay and Jennifer, who were willing to forgive their father for all of the times that I wasn't there, and for the times that I was there and yet was still able to make their lives unpleasant. They are two wonderful kids who actually want to spend time with their dad. There is an emotional bond between us that can never be broken. I had the gift of my son-in-law, Mike, and our grandson, Lucian, the next generation who has been blessed from the very beginning with loving parents and grandparents (on both sides of the family). He will have the privilege of knowing and having Jesus Christ in his life and the people around him who will always love him for who he is and not for who they think he is supposed to be.

The amazing gift of Grace—the most beautiful, spectacular, awe inspiring, and still unbelievable gift that was given to me freely, the moment I accepted Christ into my life. I sit here today, looking out the window, and still wonder at the magnificence of how Jesus humbled Himself to come into our world and take all of our sins onto His shoulders. I think about how He allowed grace to enter into our lives, and how He allowed grace to enter into my life.

I was given the gift of having my life transformed, and was able to put aside my pride and selfishness, replacing them with the outpouring of grace into others' lives. I was able to take that which was given to me—a second chance at life—and live it according to His plan, not mine. I have the gift of loving, caring for, and respecting Janet, as she has me. I have my children to love, care for, and respect, as they have me. My two-year-old grandson, Lucian, gives me the gift of his example. I can treat others as he does: with pure honesty, respect, and an outpouring of love.

God's grace has not only been what has changed my life, it has been what has saved my life. My job now is to pour that grace out onto everyone else around me.

"Between here and heaven, every minute that a Christian lives will be a minute of grace."
- Charles Spurgeon

Epilogue

"Come to me, all you who are weary and burdened, and I will give you rest. Take my yoke upon you and learn from me, for I am gentle and humble in heart, and you will find rest for your souls. For my yoke is easy and my burden is light."

Matthew 11:28-30

In the dictionary, the definition for the word, 'come,' is 'to move from a place thought of as there to, or into, a place thought of as here.' Jesus is telling us in the verse above, from the book of Matthew, that all of us who are weary and burdened should come to Him and He will give us rest. Jesus frees us from all of our burdens. He came down from heaven, humbled Himself to be with us, suffered, and died on a cross—all so that we could be freed from the burdens of this life. All that we need to do is invite Him into our hearts.

By inviting Him into my life, it changed my whole outlook on what work and relationships were all about. It was no longer about the toil, the grind and the pressure to perform. It was now about building purposeful relationships with those that I not only work with, but those in my personal life as well. It doesn't mean that the actual work becomes easier. It just means that we have someone to walk alongside us, who lightens our load, and who gives us real purpose in what we do.

He is asking us to move from the place where we all too often find ourselves: the there, which for me was an isolated, lonely, and selfish place, and come on over to the here, which is a place right next to Him. Jesus is letting us know that doing life is an arduous task in and of itself, but doing life on our own, all by ourselves, is all the more brutal. I tried for so many years to do life on my own, to make all the decisions, to be the man, to tough it out. The burdens were always there, and I always felt that I could carry them all—but I was wrong. I came to the realization that my shoulders were only so big, and so much of what was truly important in my life was falling to the wayside and being discarded. I realized that I was inadequate on my own.

This 'putting all of the weight on our own shoulders' is a challenge for anyone, but I think it can be especially challenging for men. A lot of us are taught from a very early age that we should be able to tough it out, and we should be successful—according to the world's definition of success—at whatever it is that we decide to do. "Real men" don't need any help. We learn to hold in our emotions and try not to show weakness of any kind. This is what was pounded into me from an early age. I was not going to look weak and was not going to ask for help from anybody. And I didn't for so long—and almost lost it all.

It took the Grace of God and the redemption of the Holy Spirit on that cold, crisp day in 2008 to finally bring me to my knees—to allow God to take all of the burdens that I had been trying to carry all by myself for all of those years and lift them off of my shoulders. It took accepting Jesus into my life to finally get me to quit living only with my head and to start living and loving from my heart. It took a radical transformation.

The road has not been easy, and there is—and always will be—a lot of work yet to do. The walls that had been up for so many years are coming down one at a time. Back then, there was a reason for those walls, a logical reason. I had a lot of pain and suffering in my life that needed to be contained, and those walls were a good way of hiding all of that from everyone else. I needed the kudos and the pats on the back from those around me to make myself feel proud, and keeping those walls intact was the only way that was going to happen.

Now that those walls are falling away and Jesus has rescued me from the pain, my heart is free to love. My heart is free to give my wife a warm embrace and to be able to ask her for help—help with my job, help with my kids, help with my walk with Christ. I am free to let her know that she is my best friend and that I could not do life without her. To let her know the comfort that I now feel because we are on this journey and that God has yoked the two of us together forever.

I am free to be able to love my children the way that children should be loved, to give them a hug and to speak the words, "I love you," as if telling them for the first time, to be able to encourage my daughter and son-in-law, and to open up and share with them some of the turmoil and struggles that I brought on myself throughout my life—hardships that they won't have to repeat because those walls have been taken down; to be able to love and have a relationship with my grandson, Lucian, to have an active part in his life, and to be able to see him grow up with God by his side.

I am free to have a relationship with my son, to be able to sit next to him, put my arm around him, and tell him that I am proud of him—proud of him for who he is, and not for someone that I want him to be. God is working in both of our hearts and allowing the two of us to change the generational pattern that was established long ago with the men in our family. He is allowing us to love each other unconditionally. It has been a hard journey for the two of us and will be something that we will both have to work on for the rest of our lives, but having God right there at our side I know that the healing will continue.

***

God has transformed my work life as well. He has not only allowed The Shoe Shine Guys to grow as a company, but for me to grow right along with it. Walking with Jesus does not mean that you cannot have a successful job or career. Being successful is not wrong. What were wrong were my motives. I had put my job and my career above everything else. What I needed, and a big reason for stepping away from my previous career, was to change how I prioritized my work. My work before Christ was the main focus of my life. I looked for success. I longed for success. I did everything I needed to do to be successful. The problem was that it was all about me. My priorities have now changed and work is now about what I can do for the Glory of the Lord. Colossians 3:23 – "Whatever you do, work at it with all your heart, as working for the Lord, not for men."

God has allowed me, through this new adventure called The Shoe Shine guys, to redefine what 10 Bits of Wisdom represent. I can understand now that my (1) purpose is not all about me and what I can get out of life, but is about bringing Glory to God on a daily basis and representing the face of Jesus in everything that I do. It is about refining my (2) character and continually putting integrity and honor at the forefront of every decision that I make. It is about bringing the right (3) attitude to the table no matter what the circumstances, or however high the cards are stacked up against me.

God has allowed me to better understand, through The Shoe Shine Guys, that it is important to set (4) goals and to build (5) teamwork and trust, not only with those that I work with, but with my customers as well. He has shown me that having (6) respect for all others is a fundamental principle of a walk with Christ, and that having the (7) courage to do that, while not always easy, will allow you to strengthen your commitment to Christ, and be able to stand firm in your faith.

God has taken the last of the three bits of wisdom, (8) regrets, (9) reconciliation, and (10) grace, and stripped me of the hardened exterior that I used to define myself by. He has opened up my heart and soul to what it really means to work and be of service to others. I am able to not think about the mistakes of the past or worry about the next bad decision I will end up making. Reconciliation and Grace have become as much a part of my working world as they are in my personal relationships. I am able to forgive when a wrong has been done, to ask for forgiveness when coming up short, and to extend grace to all.

The Shoe Shine Guys is now a place of business where Janet and John Shay and I work together as a family. We have trucks out on the road and a storefront shoe repair shop. But it's not just about shining and fixing shoes for the masses—it's about building relationships with all of those that we come into contact with, and about touching lives in a way that only God could have made possible. My wife and I pray for our customers every day. We will continue to grow as the good Lord sees fit and continue to follow the direction of His will.

***

Finally, how do I feel about all that has happened in my life over the last seven years or so, since that drive east on I-696 that changed my life forever? It's hard to put into words the feelings that go through my mind when I think of what God has done in my life. I will start with the fact that I now actually have feelings! It amazes me to this day that I can cry, and laugh, and love, and hope, and sing praise, and worship—with feelings and emotions that were all foreign to me for so long.

God has given me a new life. He has renewed my mind and my heart and my soul. He has blessed not only me, but my family and everyone around me, because He has transformed my life and brought me to the place where I was always meant to be. That place is here, and not there. He has brought me next to Him.

Matthew 7:7-8 – "Ask and it will be given to you; seek and you will find; knock and the door will be opened to you. For everyone who asks, receives; he who seeks, finds; and to him who knocks, the door will be opened."

Acknowledgments

This book was something that I had been thinking about for a long time; unfortunately, procrastination is one of my personality traits, so I really need to say thank you to Barbara Terry and the Waldorf Publishing team for reaching out to me when they did. God always brings people into our lives for very specific reasons, and always at just the right time. Thank you, Barbara, for contacting me and for walking me through this process. It has been an awesome experience to work with you and your group.

Thank you to Jahnavi Newsome for helping with the editing of this book and for making sure that my sentences didn't run on and on and on.....which I have a tendency to do if not held in check. To Bre, a special friend to both Janet and I, who is always there to help and who has spent countless hours on my Blog over the last couple of years. Her advice and feedback on this book were invaluable.

A big thank you to four of my friends and brothers in Christ - Alex, Tim, Bob, and Dale - who took the time to read the book and give me the encouragement to continue writing and to complete the task. The same goes to all those who have read my Blog over the last couple of years and who took the time to send me their comments. Thank you all for sharing your stories and for inspiring me.

A big thank you, a warm hug, and a sincere "I love you" to Janet, John Shay, Jennifer, Mike, and Lucian. Without all of you, none of this would have been possible. Thank you for standing by me and praying for me all those years. Your prayers were heard.

Thank you to my Lord and Savior, Jesus Christ. For knocking me down off of that high horse and for picking me up and transforming my life. Through Him all things really are possible.

Author Bio

John moved to Houston, Texas, in 1980 at the age of 21. He worked in sales for a manufacturer's rep firm selling oil equipment. His sales territory was most of south Texas, driving 4000-5000 miles per month. John had the opportunity to call on customers that were located in remote areas of south Texas as well as the corporate offices of some of the largest oil and gas companies in the world located in Houston, Texas.

In 1986, he moved back to Michigan and went to work as a mortgage consultant for a small mortgage company, Tranex Financial, and worked there for 13 years. Starting out as a mortgage consultant, he moved into training then became an officer of the company and eventually bought the firm. In 1998, he merged Tranex into the Hantz Financial Group.

He worked with Hantz Financial as a Vice President and financial consultant until December of 2010, focusing on marketing and client relationships. His team assisted high net worth clients with their tax planning, estate planning, investment strategies, and business owner concerns, providing advice to clients who needed sophisticated financial planning. While at Hantz Financial, the company grew from 100 employees to over 500 and John was able to help build one of the largest practices within the firm.

In April of 2011 he created The Shoe Shine Guys, a mobile shoe shine service that started with an idea, one truck, and a handful of clients. He now has three vehicles, a full-service cobbler store and hundreds of clients. His company continues to add new clients every month and receive calls at least once a quarter about expanding to other parts of the country.

John and his wife of 33 years, Janet, have two grown children, John Shay and Jennifer; one son-in-law, Mike; and one rambunctious and adorable grandson, Lucian. A sports enthusiast, John was an avid handball player for over 20 years (a new titanium knee and work have sidelined him for a while) and was the Canadian national doubles champion in 1999.

Reference Page

Anka, P. (Composer). (1968). "I Did It My Way." [F. Sinatra, Performer] Los Angeles, CA, USA.

Carnegie, D. (1936). *How to Win Friends and Influence People*. New York City: Simon and Schuster.

Covey, S. (1989). *The 7 Habits of Highly Effective People*. New York: Free Press.

Frankl, V. E. (1946). *Man's Search For Meaning*. London: Rider Books.

Kendall, R. T. (2004). *Total Forgiveness Experience*. Lake Mary: Charisma House.

Lencioni, P. (2002). *The Five Dysfunctions of a Team*. Manhattan: Jossey-Bass.

Melville, H. (1851). *Moby Dick*. New York: Harper& Brothers.

Nee, W. (1957). *The Normal Christian Life*. Bombay: Gospel Literature Service.

Ortbert, J. (2007). *When The Game Is Over, It All Goes Back In The Box*. Grand Rapids: Zondervan.

Roosevelt, T. (1899). *The Strenuous Life*. Chicago.

Sittser, J. (2009). *A Grace Disguised: How The Soul Grows Through Loss*. Grand Rapids: Zondervan.

Solzhenitsyn, A. (1967). *Cancer Ward*. New York City: Dial Press.

Spurgeon, C. (1909, March 25). "SOUL SATISFACTION." London, UK: Charles Spurgeon.

Tiegreen, C. (2007). *The One Year Walk with God Devotional*. Carol Stream: Tyndale House Publishers, Inc.

Tutu, A. D. (2009). *No Future Without Forgiveness*. New York: Crown Publishing Group.

Ware, B. (2012). *The Top Five Regrets of the Dying: A Life Transformed by the Dearly Departing*. London: Hay House.

Warren, R. (2002). *The Purpose Driven-Life: What On Earth Am I Here For?* Grand Rapids: Zondervan.